THE
VILLAGE
PARLIAMENTS

THE
VILLAGE
PARLIAMENTS

The Centenary of West Sussex
ParishCouncils, 1994

Valerie Porter

Published for

west sussex county council

by

Phillimore

1994

Published by
PHILLIMORE & CO. LTD.
for West Sussex County Council
Shopwyke Manor Barn, Chichester, Sussex

© West Sussex County Council, 1994

ISBN 0 85033 894 8

Printed and bound in Great Britain by
BIDDLES LTD.
Guildford, Surrey

Contents

List of Illustrations

List of Tables

List of Maps

Acknowledgements

This book could not have been written without the active participation of the many West Sussex parish clerks and parish councillors (past and present) who have taken a great deal of trouble to research their own archives. Though it has not been possible to include more than a fraction of their material, their enthusiasm and diligence are reflected in the pages of the book. They are too numerous to mention individually, as are others who contributed items about their parishes to the pages of *The Clerk* (the quarterly Journal of the Society of Local Council Clerks, edited from Sussex for many years by Roy Gibbs).

There are several other people whose considerable help has been invaluable. I am particularly grateful to John Godfrey (Assistant County Secretary) and West Sussex County Council for wholeheartedly supporting this project, and to Kim Leslie and all the staff at the West Sussex Record Office for their courtesy, expertise and imaginative delving. Martin Hayes opened the doors to the wealth of parish information at Worthing Library and in fact throughout the West Sussex County library service. The history of the county's roads was revealed by Maurice Milne (once the County's Surveyor), Dennis Bostwick (County's Traffic department), Phil Henty (Signs section) and Gerald Nutbeem (at Amberley Chalkpits Museum). Finally, the support of Noel Osborne and Phillimore & Co Ltd as publishers of the book has been vital.

Illustration Acknowledgements

The illustrations appear by kind permission of the following: B. Marjorie Baldwin, 12 (Colgate Parish Magazine, 1894), 47 (*The Story of the Forest,* 1985); Bognor Regis Local History Society (Ken Scutt), 17; Burgess Hill Town Council, 56; Mrs. P. Calderwood, 81; Les Coker, 50; Margaret Cornford, 100; Martin Cornford, 98, 99, 101; Inez Dann, 73; Eastergate Parish Council, 42; Ian Grant, 79; Henfield Parish Council/Museum, 11, 29, 57, 77, 78; John Hill, 87; Ken Hughes, 52, 74; H. R. Jarmaine (Execs. for Fanny Hole), 71, 72; Kim Leslie, 4, 9, 23, 31, 41, 63, 75, 84; Lynchmere Parish Council, 93; Keith Nethercoate-Bryant, 59; David Nicholls, 1-3, 34, 43, 44, 48, 53, 54, 58, 69, 80, 85, 88-90, 94; Patching and Clapham Parish Councils, 95-97; Valerie Porter, 46, 91; Portsmouth Publishing & Printing Ltd., 92; Mrs. Bertha Stewart Watson, 25, 76; Stoughton Parish Council, 38; *Sussex County Magazine*, Vol. 1 (1927), 49; Mary Taylor, 33; Twineham Parish Council, 22; Conrad Volk, 82, 83; WSRO parish records, 13-16, 18-21, 28, 40, 86; WSRO Garland collection, 6-7, 10, 24, 26, 27, 32, 35-37, 39, 60, 61, 64, 66-68, 70; WSRO photo collection, 5, 30, 62, 65; WSRO, 8, 45, 51.

Introduction

Parish councils form the lowest tier of local government and that is their secret strength. They are the foundation stones of the whole system and their rôle is the most ancient. They operate wholeheartedly at the grass roots and are, at the very least, vital barometers of their parishes' needs and opinions. Their rôle, though it has changed in detail over the years, has always been based on looking after the interests of the parish—its inhabitants and its environment.

The elected members of a parish council, and the clerk who serves it, are recognisable and named individuals who live and often work within the community they represent, and therefore they take a personal interest: the actions of the parish council directly affect the lives of its councillors as well as those of the rest of the parish. Between them, parish councillors know everybody in the parish and they know what goes on there, on a day-to-day basis—all the little niggles of local life. They *know*, because they are on the spot. The best of them watch, listen and respond immediately, or even anticipate.

As monitors, they are often frustrated by a lack of real power to sort out parish problems themselves, but they can and do seek action and support from the next levels of local government— the district and county councils. It is worth remembering, in those moments of frustration, that there are far, far more elected parish councillors than county and district councillors.

But parish councils can also take action themselves, by their own initiatives; that is to say, they can inspire local schemes and then involve everyone in the parish in carrying them out for themselves. That is the essence of parish life—the nurturing of a true community spirit in which people actually do something about it rather than leaving it to 'them'.

****

This book, published with the help of West Sussex County Council in support of its new 'Statement of Partnership' with its local councils, shows how the parish councils evolved from a much older form of local government and how they were expected to be exciting and revolutionary. The story of their subsequent development was, frankly, one of considerable disappointment until the Second World War revived a sense of involvement in the local community and a vigour for the villagers to help themselves again. That vigour has received a fresh boost in recent years and many West Sussex parish councils have become what some like to call 'proactive'. Often under the guidance of a better trained and sometimes younger clerk than traditionally, and with greater inspiration and imagination among the councillors themselves, the parish councils are pumping life back into communities that were quietly losing identity and heart.

There is a new spirit of enterprise among many parish councils in this county and a large number of them have co-operated in the writing of this book by contributing a wealth of detailed information about their past and present along with some invaluable illustrations, though it has

1

1. *(Above left)* In session: Warnham Parish Council, October 1993.

2. *(Above right)* & 3 *(Below Left)* Partnership in action. West Sussex County Council supports local projects through its Parish Council Initiatives Fund. County councillor Michael Dennis hands a cheque to Mrs. Joy Lambert, chairman of Horsted Keynes Parish Council, for the restoration of the clapperboards in Freshfield Lane in 1993. This traditional raised walkway becomes essential when the River Ouse floods here.

3. Supporting the Selsey-County Link. The people of Selsey now have direct access to County Hall, Chichester, through a dedicated telephone/fax line installed in 1993. From left to right: Fred Robertson (clerk to Selsey Parish Council), Peter Ogden (county and parish councillor), Mike Beal (chairman, Selsey Parish Council), Michael Hancock (Assistant to the Chief Executive, West Sussex County Council).

only been possible to include a fraction of the rich store of material they have researched. Their centenary year is an appropriate one in which to celebrate this rebirth and the aim of the book is to encourage every parish in the county to sit up, freshen up, take notice and *act*. If the will is there, it can be done, whatever the real or imaginary obstacles. We owe that much to the original visionaries who created the parish councils in 1894.

Chapter One

Back Along

The root of the word 'parish' is from the Greek: *para*, beside, and *oikos*, a dwelling (the Greek word *paroika* today implies a colony or quarter). The parish is the oldest and most stable district of civil administration in England, preceding the manorial system by several centuries. In many cases, parish boundaries remain almost identical to those at the time of Domesday Book, and before, although there has been an alarming tendency to tamper with them in the last century or two.

****

Sussex, which had been the old kingdom of the South Saxons, was the first to feel the boot-heel of the conquering Normans in 1066. In the Domesday Survey it was uniquely divided into rapes —large districts running from the coast up to its northern boundary, each dominated by a lord based at a castle not far from that coast, and protecting it. The rapes were named after their castles.

Like other counties, Sussex was also divided into hundreds, and these were divided into parishes, many of which in Sussex seemed to reflect the north/south lie of the rapes. In several parts of West Sussex, as the old maps show, bunches of the parishes were extraordinarily long and narrow in outline. Such a stretched shape ensured that each parish included a range of environmental resources—pasture and arable, woodland and meadow, upland and valley and so on. Sadly the agricultural essence of rural parishes has been diluted and most of them have lost their ancient shape in revisions of the parishes during the past two centuries.

Table 1 shows how the parishes were grouped into the ancient rapes and hundreds.

****

Long before the Norman invasion, the church had begun to make its mark and to extract its dues from laymen in a plethora of alms, scots and tithes. It was natural that, when the time came to delineate the area from which such dues were collected and ministrations made, the churches adopted existing boundaries of the original parishes, some of which pre-dated even the Romans. Here and there, ancient yew trees or sarsen stones or other markers still suggest evidence of the pre-Christian definition of parish boundaries. (When did your parishioners last walk their bounds?) The old parishes became ecclesiastical units, and would remain so in contrast to the worldly Norman manors until 1894.

The Church established a system whereby every inhabitant who belonged to the parish church could be summoned annually to meet in a parish assembly in order to raise and apportion the church rates and to elect the churchwardens who were responsible for collecting the rate and carrying out other parochial business such as maintaining the fabric of the church. Thus the Elizabethan legislators found a very handy organisation already in existence for the collection and allotment of local taxes, and they used it as the basis for the implementation of the Poor Relief Act 1601, effectively re-establishing the parish as a civil unit although it was formally still seen as an ecclesiastical one. The law made the churchwardens responsible for the parish's poor; the parish was to appoint Overseers of the Poor and must raise a local tax, the poor rate, from every householder. The whole parish, churchgoing or not, was directly involved in looking after its own disadvantaged: the poor, the old, the widowed, the orphaned, the illegitimate and the sick—people known as individuals, with personal histories and names and faces. Today we have lost that direct sense of caring, in the tendency to let the Welfare State, in all its anonymity, take the responsibility for them instead.

Table 1   Ancient (civil) parishes by hundreds and rapes

RAPE OF ARUNDEL		RAPE OF BRAMBER	
HUNDRED	**PARISH**	**HUNDRED**	**PARISH**
Arundel	Arundel		Clapham
Avisford	Barnham		Durrington
	Binsted		Findon
	Climping		Heene
	Eastergate		Lancing
	Felpham		Sompting
	Ford	Burbeach	Beeding, Upper
	Madehurst		Beeding, Upper
	Middleton		Beeding, Lower
	Stoke, South		Edburton
	Tortington		Ifield
	Walberton	East Easwrith	Itchingfield
	Yapton		Sullington
Bury	Alfold (part)		Thakeham
	Bignor		Warminghurst
	Bury	Fishergate	Kingston-by-Sea
	Coates		Shoreham, New
	Coldwaltham		Shoreham, Old
	Fittleworth		Southwick
	Hardham	Patching	Patching
	Houghton	Singlecross	Horsham
Poling	Angmering		Nuthurst
	Burpham		Rusper
	Ferring		Warnham
	Goring	Steyning	Bramber
	Kingston		Botolphs
	Lyminster		Coombes
	Lyminster		Steyning
	Warningcamp		Washington
	Littlehampton		Wiston
	Poling	Tarring	Tarring, West
	Preston, East	Tipnoak	Albourne
	Rustington		Henfield
	Stoke, North		Woodmancote
Rotherbridge	Barlavington	West Grinstead	Ashington
	Burton		Ashurst
	Duncton		Grinstead, West
	Egdean		Shipley
	Kirdford	Windham & Ewhurst	Cowfold
	Lurgashall		Shermanbury
	North Chapel		
	Petworth		
	Stopham		
	Sutton		
	Tillington		
	Woolavington		
West Easwrith	Amberley		
	Amberley		
	Rackham Hamlet		
	Billingshurst		
	Chiltington, West		
	Greatham		
	Parham		
	Pulborough		
	Rudgwick		
	Slinfold		
	Storrington		
	Wiggonholt		
Brightford	Broadwater		

RAPE OF CHICHESTER

HUNDRED	PARISH
Aldwick	Bersted, South
	Bersted, South
	Bognor
	Lavant, East
	Pagham
	Slindon
	The Gumber
	Tangmere
Bosham	Bosham
	Chidham
	Funtington
	Stoke, West
	Thorney, West
Box & Stockbridge	Aldingbourne
	Appledram
	Boxgrove
	Donnington
	Eartham
	Fishbourne, New
	Hunston
	Merston
	Mundham, North
	Oving
	Rumboldswyke
	Up Waltham
	West Hampnett
Dumpford	Bramshot (part)
	Chithurst
	Didling
	Elsted
	Harting
	Rogate
	Terwick
	Treyford
	Trotton
Easebourne	Bepton
	Cocking
	Easebourne
	Farnhurst
	Graffham
	Heyshott
	Iping
	Linch
	Linchmere
	Lodsworth
	Midhurst
	Selham
	Stedham
	Steep (part)
	Ambersham, North
	Ambersham, South
	Woolbeding
Manhood	Birdham
	Earnley
	Itchenor, West
	Selsey
	Sidlesham
	Wittering, East
	Wittering, West

RAPE OF CHICHESTER (cont.)

HUNDRED	PARISH
Westbourne & Singleton	Binderton
	Compton
	Dean, East
	Dean, West
	Marden, East
	Marden, North
	Mid Lavant
	Racton
	Singleton
	Stoughton
	Up Marden
	Westbourne

RAPE OF LEWES*

HUNDRED	PARISH
Buttinghill	Ardingly
	Balcombe
	Bolney
	Clayton
	Crawley
	Cuckfield
	Hoathly, West
	Hurstpierpoint
	Keymer
	Slaugham
	Twineham
	Worth
Poynings	Edburton (part)
	Fulking Hamlet
	Newtimber
	Poynings
	Pyecombe

RAPE OF PEVENSEY*

HUNDRED	PARISH
Burleigh Arches	Lindfield
Danehill Horsted	Horsted Keynes
East Grinstead	East Grinstead

City of Chichester*

* Indicates that part which was transferred to West Sussex from East Sussex.

Hundreds etc as subsequent to 1844 Act (7 & 8 Vict.)

Source: *Victoria County History, Sussex*, Vol. 2 (Comparative population tables 1801-1901)

1. Speed's map of Sussex, 1610.

The Vestry Meeting

Churches were often the only buildings in which people could convene indoors (there was a long tradition of outdoor meetings in the style of what could be called village councils) and therefore became natural meeting places at which all sorts of local matters, not necessarily ecclesiastical or concerning the Poor Laws, could be sorted out by the people of the parish. The parson's annual meetings began to take decisions about thoroughly unspiritual but essential local matters such as making and mending the parish's roads and appointing various local officers, including their own parish constables to keep the peace locally. **Upper Beeding**, for example, nominated a wheelwright, a baker, a labourer and a smith to serve as parish constable in 1859 and continued to make its annual nominations until a new parliamentary Act of 1872 made such appointments no longer compulsory. This parish at first decided, perhaps with relief, that it was no longer 'expedient' to elect parish constables but it soon asked its Overseers to 'call the attention of the Authorities, or the Justices, to the very inefficient Police protection to the property belonging to the outlying districts of the Parish specially at Night-time and respectfully requesting the same may be remedied'. The following year Upper Beeding reverted to nominating its four men again and continued to do so for several years. Many a parish recorded its purchase of new pairs of handcuffs, or the parish constable's attempts to arrest 'putative fathers' and serve them with bastardy orders, as well as escorting prisoners to the nearest town jail or confining one to the parish's own one-man lock-up.

The parishioners usually met in the church vestry and thus their gatherings came to be known as Vestry meetings. Those who attended what was called the 'open' Vestry meeting each year included the poor as well as the rich, and women as well as men—a much broader 'franchise' than any other form of government at the time.

The Vestry meetings were the immediate forerunners of the parish councils. The old Vestry minutes—many examples of which have been lodged with the West Sussex Record Office in Chichester—give a flavour of the wide range of activities that they covered and a most vivid picture of daily life in the parish right up to 1894. Table 2 gives a taste and should send anybody with a real interest in local history scurrying to the West Sussex Record Office for a look at the Vestry archives. Many people, incidentally, found the vestry itself far too cold, draughty and damp or simply too small for their meetings and promptly adjourned—usually to the local inn. **Balcombe** Vestry, for example, met at the *Half Moon*; **Bolney** divided their time between the *Eight Bells* and the *Race Horse Inn*; it was the *King's Head* or the *Rising Sun* for **Upper Beeding**, and either the *White Horse*, the *Half Moon* or the schoolroom for **Storrington**'s Vestry. **Rudgwick**, in 1833, resolved to end their Vestry meetings with 'a Dinner and Two Glasses'.

Table 2. The Vestry Meeting: a random sample of subjects

Parish appointments:	Poor Law matters:
Overseers and Assistant Overseers	Workhouse
Highway Surveyors	Parish cottages
Parish Constables	Poor House cottages
Waywardens	Almshouses
Assessors	Clothing
Charity Trustees	Potatoes
Churchwardens	Bread and flour
Parish Valuers	Nursing
Parish Doctors	Vagrants
Parish Medical Officers	Occupations for paupers
Schoolmasters	London Truss Society for Relief of
Guardians	Ruptured Poor

Highways etc.:
Road duty
Parish labour
Parish teams (draught animals)
Parish cart-house
Bridges
Stone, scalpings etc
Sale of manure by waywardens
Footpaths
Flooding
Ponds
Drainage
Stonebreaking

Other:
Fire brigade
Burial grounds
New schools
Apprenticeships
Emigration and colonisation
Beershops
Pub raids
Smallpox precautions
Treading the bounds
Rating assessments
Crying a notice (against stealing wood)
Price for sparrow eggs and heads
Bastardy payments
Parish handcuffs
Rewards re criminals
Constable's bills for various duties
Parish pounds
Reading-rooms
Recreation grounds

This system jogged along in quite an informal way but was already crumbling during the 18th century, when the overseers, with their substantial local knowledge, became more and more dominated by the distant JPs. The parishes had been empowered to purchase or hire workhouses for the poor but were being encouraged to combine with other parishes for the purpose as it was considered that larger units would be more efficient and economic. The Poor Law Amendment

4.   Former parish workhouse at Steyning, photographed in the 1920s.

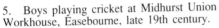
5.   Boys playing cricket at Midhurst Union
Workhouse, Easebourne, late 19th century.

6.   Inside Petworth Workhouse, 1930.

Act of 1834 precipitated the creation of Boards of Guardians in charge of groups or unions of
parishes which, while they were sometimes based on old hundreds boundaries, more often were
not: history was not considered important and, like the redrawn maps of colonial Africa, the new
union boundaries owed more to geographical and administrative convenience, often disregarding
traditional affinities and strongly voiced local opposition.

The result was that the old Vestry, representing the parish, found its direct responsibility
for its own poor being taken over by more distant authorities. It also found that the voices of
its less fortunate parishioners became unheard as the Vestry lost its powers to the Board of
Guardians. Then there developed a positive plethora of boards for this, that and the other,
increasing the feeling of centralisation and the lack of faith in the parish to run its own affairs.
The parish, which had traditionally looked after its own problems on behalf of all its inhabitants
with minimal interference, was now being told what to do by people who did not even live within
its boundaries.

The legislators had the bit between their teeth but their ideals often stumbled at local level.
The Boards of Guardians became overwhelmed by a whole series of new laws on public health
and nuisances, and the locals became thoroughly bewildered by randomly created areas of
jurisdiction for this and that, their boundaries not necessarily related to each other nor even to
county boundaries. The overlapping created a chaotic network and no one really knew which
district they were in for what purpose.

To sort it all out, a Royal Sanitary Commission was appointed in 1868 and its report three
years later proposed single authorities in the towns, and the Poor Law Unions as administrative
districts in the rural areas under the authority of the Guardians. It was considered that the parishes
themselves had become too creaky and inefficient to be a useful element of the administrative
machinery. The rural Boards of Guardians became Rural Sanitary Authorities when the Public
Health Act came into effect in 1875; they would in due course become the basis of rural district
councils.

Amid all this legislation and confusion, the once active Vestry quietly slipped into
insignificance, with hardly any administrative rôle in its own parish. But its Overseers still raised
local revenues: they issued precepts, they evaluated local properties for their rating books and
they kept a register of qualified voters in the parish. The Vestry still nominated them and
appointed their paid assistants, but did very little else. The village voices were fading in apathy,
and everything was being left to 'them'.

They were bewildered but not wholly beaten. In the 1870s the Liberal party, under
Goschen, declared that it wanted to give the 'peasants' a real interest in rural administration, and

a proper influence over it as well. The party line was that the parish should be given fresh life: the creation of a new democratic organisation based on the parish was a primary plank in the Liberal programme.

Goschen proposed to reconstitute the parish entirely. In 1871 he said:

> There should be in every parish what I will call a 'civil head', a person who shall be responsible for the affairs of that parish. We propose that the ratepayers in every parish should annually elect from themselves a person to be called Chairman of the Parochial Board, and that he shall be associated with a certain number of other members of the Parochial Board, varying from three to twenty, according to the population of the parish, and that to this regularly constituted body, the Parochial Board, should be transferred the duties now exercised by the overseers, by the highway supervisors, by the lighting and watching inspectors and the executive duties of the Vestry, such as those which it now possesses as a sanitary authority.

7.   Jimmy Puttock, who worked on the same farm at Balls Cross, near Petworth, for more than 60 years. He was typical of those whom Gladstone wanted to realise the principles, obligations and benefits of local government.

The Bill of that year never reached its second reading but the Liberals clung to the idea. Gladstone, when the Local Government Act 1888 had created county councils, was angry that no district or parish councils had been established: we must, he cried, 'go still nearer to the door of the masses of the people' and 'avail ourselves of the old parochial division of the country, and to carry home to the mind of the peasants and the agricultural labourers the principles and the obligations, and to secure fully to them the benefits, of local government.' He continued to call for the formation of parish councils, and his intention, bluntly, was to swing the balance of power out of the centuries-old grasp of the squire and the parson and into that of the working villagers and agricultural labourers. Now that was a truly revolutionary idea, and it excited great enthusiasm among the latter.

On 2 March 1893 Sir Henry Fowler, president of Gladstone's Local Government Board, introduced the Parish and District Councils Bill. It quickly became known as the Parish Councils Bill (the idea of Districts was much less appealing). The first principle of the Bill was stated to be the introduction of *self-government* into rural parishes, by giving larger ones their own Parish Councils elected by universal suffrage of rate-paying inhabitants (including women, it should be noted) and in smaller parishes there would be Parish Meetings, of all inhabitant ratepayers, with almost the same duties and powers as the parish councils.

The Bill provoked much opposition but it received Royal assent at last on 5 March 1894, to come into effect on 17 December. The parish councils were born to the sound of a brave fanfare:

> The stability of the State is secured by the participation of all its citizens in the common life. As with the national Parliament, so with the local councils. They are elected by the people of the locality; they work under the censorship of local opinion. These little parliaments of the

county, the town, and the village, like the great Parliament of the nation, employ paid officers
to execute their commands ... At last class rule, in so far as it rested on laws and constitution,
has been totally abolished; and England has created for herself 'Self Government' in the true
sense of the word ... the right of her people to legislate, to deliberate, and to administer through
councils or parliaments elected on the basis of popular suffrage ...

The president of the National Liberal Federation proclaimed that the Act would:

abolish patronage and banish privilege. For the rule of the few it will substitute the responsibility
and co-operation of the many, it is the Charter of the peasants' liberty ... which recognised that
our country's future is safest and the common weal best insured when entrusted to the care of
all her people.

What a challenge! What great ambitions! Whatever happened?

Chapter 2

Birth

The pamphleteers went wild when the parish councils were born in 1894. In a splendid one entitled *Villagers' Magna Charta - the Village for the Villagers*, barrister J. Morrison Davidson proclaimed to his 'Brothers, Sons of the Soil':

> At last, in 1884, it was discovered by Mr Gladstone and the Liberal Party that you, the rural toilers of the land, were 'capable citizens', two millions strong, and, after a tussle with the House of Landlords, your deadly foe time out of mind, you also obtained your rights as men and citizens. With what result? A rain of County Councils, District Councils, and, most important of all, if you learn how to take full advantage of them, Parish Councils. It is a 'far cry' to Westminster and Parliament, but the Parish Council brings self-government to your very thresholds ...
>
> For the first time in your lives you will very soon have an opportunity of showing your ability to conduct your own local affairs in your own way, without the aid of Squire, Parson, or even Farmer ...

The main point of the barrister's long pamphlet was to overcome the 'bamboozlement' of all the legal phraseology and bureaucratic thinking that might confuse the average parishioner. He went into considerable detail to explain in plain English the practicalities of the Parish Councils Act when it came into effect.

> You, the new rulers of rural England, will then have to master, to the best of your ability, the affairs of
>   1. The Parish
>   2. The District
>   3. The County
> These all form parts of a grand whole, surmounted by
>   4. The Local Government Board in London.
>
> A *Parish* is 'a place for which a separate *Poor Rate* is or can be made, or for which a separate *Overseer* is or can be appointed.'
>   A *District* is either
>   1. *Rural*, or
>   2. *Urban*.
> The *Rural District* will, as far as possible, consist of the number of Parishes comprised in the old *Poor Law Unions*, lying in the same County. But, where a Parish, at present, lies partly in a *Rural*, and partly in an *Urban District*, the rural portion will be separated from the urban and become a rural parish of itself. It will be for the County Council to see that there is no overlapping.
>   The *Urban District* will be confined to strictly Borough areas, and those formerly under Local Boards and Improvement Commissions.

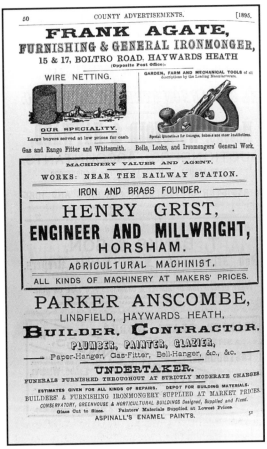

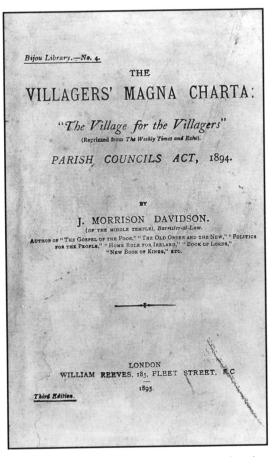

8. *(Above left)* Trade advertisements in *Kelly's Directory for Sussex*, 1895. Its publication was delayed that year because of the need to include information about the new parish councils and their clerks.

9. *(Above right)* The front of J. Morrison Davidson's *The Villagers' Magna Charta* which explained the 1894 Act in simple language for the 'Sons of the Soil'.

The *Sunday Graphic* also reviewed in depth the powers and duties of the new parish and district councils, beginning its major article in 1894 thus:

> On Tuesday, December 4th, will be held in every one of the thirteen thousand rural parishes of England and Wales a statutory meeting to decide whether the parish shall have a council, and if so who shall be elected to it. In the case of many parishes, the former of these two questions will not arise. The Local Government Act of 1894, commonly known as the Parish Councils Act, prescribes that every rural parish with a population of more than 300 persons shall, willy nilly, have a parish council. There are about 7,000 such parishes ... In these parishes, as well as in the smaller parishes, the meeting on December 4th is a meeting of all the 'electors' of the parish. Practically that means all householders and all lodgers living in the parish ...
>
> The first duty of the parochial electors is to attend the parish meeting on December 4th ... If the parish had at the census of 1891 a population of 300 or upwards, the sole duty of the meeting will be to elect a parish council... Briefly, the meeting will first elect a chairman, and the chairman will then receive nominations for the council. If only sufficient candidates are nominated to fill the places on the council, these candidates will at once be declared elected and the meeting will adjourn. If there is an excess of candidates the meeting may decide by a show of hands which persons it wishes to elect.

Any parochial elector, man or woman, married or single, is qualified to be a member of the parish council ... The first parish council elected will remain in office till March 1896; after that the elections will be annual.

After the parish council has been chosen, or a poll for its election demanded, the first meeting under the Act will come to an end. But the chairman who had been elected to preside over the meeting will still remain, as it were, in office, and will have to perform the duty of summoning the first meeting of the parish council. If no poll is demanded, the councillors elected at the parish meeting on December 4th will come into office on December 13th, and, apparently, the chairman of the first meeting must convene the council for that day. If there is a poll it will have to take place on either the 15th, the 17th, the 18th, or the 19th of December, and the councillors then elected will not come into office till December 31st. Their first duty on meeting will be to elect a chairman, who will act during his year of office both as chairman of the parish council and as chairman of the parish meeting, whenever it meets.

What about parishes with a population of fewer than 300? If there were more than 100 inhabitants, the parish could choose to have a parish council, on application to the county council by the parish meeting. Those with fewer than 100 inhabitants could not have a parish council unless the county council expressly approved of their wish to have one. But in that case the Parish Meeting would anyway acquire most of the attributes of a parish council.

10. Jackie Baxter of Egdean, with helping hands: one of the 'rural toilers of the land ... the new rulers of rural England'.

As for parish councillors themselves, here was the real revolution. Morrison Davidson was quite amazed that candidacy was extended to 'any adult, *male or female, elector, or non-elector*', as long as they had resided for twelve months in the parish or within three miles of it.

> This unheard of stretch of liberality can only be classed with those 'truths that are stranger than fiction'. ... A husband and wife, both of them non-electors and non-parishioners, may thus sit in the same Parish Council!

Morrison Davidson was an ardent feminist but the idea of women on a council was a novel one for the time, and in practice very few women were voted on to parish councils until the 1920s and 1930s.

Morrison Davidson summarised, in nine brief points, the functions of the parish councillors:

1. To appoint the Overseers and Assistant Overseer.
2. To light the streets.
3. To provide a fire-engine.
4. To acquire allotments and recreation grounds.
5. To prevent the stopping of footpaths.
6. To provide village halls, libraries, baths, or wash-houses.
7. To supply the village with water from any well, spring, or stream within the parish, the landlords consenting.
8. To complain to the District Council (the Sanitary Authority) about unhealthy dwellings.
9. To deal with drains, ponds, and ditches injurious to health.

11.   Henfield High Street, 1894. Parish councillor Samuel Tobbit stands in the doorway of his shop.

In contrast, the district councils (which were created by the same 1894 Act) had four main functions:

1. To manage the Poor Law.
2. To be the Sanitary Authority.
3. To be the Highway Authority, except for main roads.
4. To be the School Attendance Authority for Voluntary Schools in districts where there are no School Boards.

The Parish Meeting

The barrister-pamphleteer put parish councils firmly in their place by declaring: 'By far the most important creation of the Parish Councils Act 1894, is not, as you might suppose, the Parish Council itself, but the Parish Meeting. The Parish Meeting will be the old Vestry at its best, with fresh powers added and trammeled no longer by any connection with the Church.'

The Parish Meeting, of course, was a meeting of everybody in the parish, should they care to attend. All parishes, whether or not they had a parish council, were entitled to hold a parish meeting and should make the most of it. They must all hold this annual meeting on 25 March, or within seven days of that date, giving due notice of the event. The meeting could be called 'to support or protest against proposals affecting the parish' and—specifically, according to Morrison Davidson—'candidates may be "heckled"'. The majority decided, subject to poll, and a poll could be demanded at any time during the meeting—by a single voter in certain important matters, otherwise with the consent of the Chairman, or by one third of those present or five of them (whichever number was the less). The chairman had a casting vote.

The powers of the Parish Meeting, whether or not there was a parish council, would be:

1. To consider 'parish affairs' in the widest sense.
2. To adopt all or any of the 'Adoptive' Acts.
3. To sanction certain expenditure, under Adoptive Acts.
4. To prevent stopping of public rights of way within the parish by councils.
5. To consent to sale or exchange of parish property.
6. To receive accounts of non-ecclesiastical parish charities.
7. To appeal to the Education Department to form or dissolve a School Board.
8. To apply to the county council to group the parish with others or to dissolve such a group.

The Parish Council.

The first election of Parish Councillors under the new Local Government Act of 1894 took place at Lower Beeding on Dec. 4th. Eleven Councillors had to be elected, and there were eighteen Candidates nominated, ten from Lower Beeding, and eight from Colgate. A show of hands was taken, and resulted in the following being chosen as the first representatives on the Parish Council for the united parishes:—W. E. Hubbard, J. Clifton-Brown, A. Gent, J. Cripps, E. Randall, J. King, R. W. Powell, J. Winser, D. Pearce, E. King, G. Sharpe. The first meeting of the Council took place at Lower Beeding on Dec. 17th, when Mr. W. E. Hubbard was elected as the Chairman for the ensuing year, Mr. F. Cripps was elected as Assistant Overseer, and Clerk to the Council.

---

12. Lower Beeding Parish Council gives notice of its first election and meeting, December 1894, in the parish magazine.

For parishes with no separate parish council, the parish meeting could also:

1. Apply to the county council to become a parish council or for a grouping order.
2. Apply to the county council for any of the powers of a parish council.
3. Appoint committees for any purpose.
4. Appoint the Overseers and appoint or remove an Assistant Overseer.
5. Appoint trustees of non-ecclesiastical parish charities in place of Overseers and Churchwardens.
6. Levy a rate not exceeding sixpence in the pound for all purposes. ('What a farce!' exclaimed our barrister. 'Why not six shillings, ye jugglers?')
7. Complain to the county council of any neglect of duty by the district council in sanitary matters.

Where there *was* a parish council, the parish meeting could or should:

1. Elect the councillors, unless a poll was demanded, when it would be for the parish electors to choose their councillors.
2. Consent or withhold consent for the parish council to incur a rate of more than threepence in the pound or involving a loan, or to sell or exchange any parish property.
3. Expect the county council to consult with the parish meeting when naming any parish.

So, the parish meeting had considerable powers over its own parish council, if there was one, and Morrison Davidson got quite excitable about choosing to remain a Parish Meeting if that was an option for a smaller parish—especially because of that clause about being able to

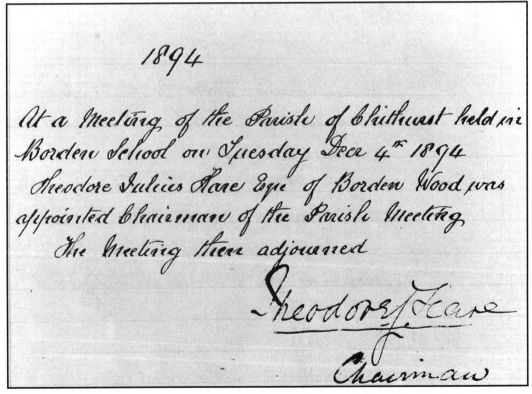

13.   Handwritten minutes of the first Parish Meeting for Chithurst on 4 December 1894—the day on which all parishes were supposed to hold a meeting. The minutes are typically brief.

THE PARISH COUNCILS ACT, 1894.

ANNUAL PARISH MEETING, 1895.

What Business can be Transacted at an Annual Assembly of the Parish Meeting. (*a*)

BY

J. WALLIS-DAVIES,

Solicitor and Secretary to the Parish and Rural District Councils Association,
16, Parliament Street, London, S.W.

N.B.—The Annual Assembly of the Parish Meeting must be held on the 25th day of March in each year, *or within seven days before or after* that day.

1. To elect Chairman if necessary (*b*).

2. To read and confirm Minutes of last Meeting.

3. Appoint Overseers (*c*).

4. Appointment or revocation of appointment of Assistant Overseers if necessary (*d*).

5. Appoint Committees if necessary (*e*).

6. Receive and peruse Accounts of all Parochial Charities (*f*).

7. Appointment of Trustees to Parochial Charities where necessary (*g*).

8. Consider the Draft of any Scheme relating to Charities (*h*).

9. Consider any proposition relative to any one or more of the Adoptive Acts (*i*).

(*a*) A Parish Meeting must be held *annually* at least in every rural parish, whether there is a Parish Council or not. Sec. 2 (1 & 3) and Sched. I., Part I., r. 1.

Note.—As to what Notice of Meetings is necessary, and by whom to be given, *see* Sched. I., Part I., rr. 2 and 3 ; Sections 51 and 45 (3).

(*b*) In parishes not having a Parish Council, the Chairman has already been appointed, and continues in office until March, 1896. Sec. 78 (3). If such a Chairman is absent, or if in parishes having a Parish Council the Chairman or Vice-Chairman be absent, then the Parish Meeting may choose their own Chairman. Sec. 2 (4).

(*c*) Overseers can be appointed by the Parish Meeting only where there is no Council. Sec. 19 (5). In parishes having a Parish Council, Overseers will be appointed by them at the Annual Meeting in April.

Notice of appointments must be sent to Guardians within three weeks. Sec. 50. Authorised and prescribed Forms of Appointment and Notices are supplied by Messrs. Eyre and Spottiswoode, Queen's Printers, London, E.C.

(*d*) In parishes not having a Parish Council. Sec. 19 (5).

(*e*) Sec. 19 (3).

(*f*) Sec. 14 (6). These accounts should be recorded in the Minute Book.

(*g*) Sec. 14. Application for guidance and advice should be made to the Association.

(*h*) Sec. 14 (5).

(*i*) Sec. 7.

p. 20.

14.   The Parish Councils Act 1894: some helpful advice.

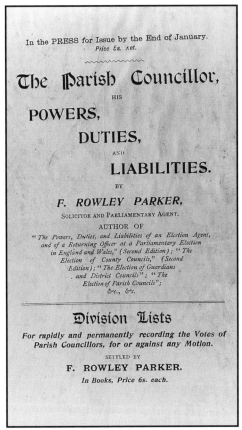

In the PRESS for Issue by the End of January.
Price 6s. net.

The Parish Councillor,

HIS

POWERS,

DUTIES,

AND

LIABILITIES.

BY

F. ROWLEY PARKER,

SOLICITOR AND PARLIAMENTARY AGENT.

AUTHOR OF

"*The Powers, Duties, and Liabilities of an Election Agent,
and of a Returning Officer at a Parliamentary Election
in England and Wales," (Second Edition); "The
Election of County Councils," (Second
Edition); "The Election of Guardians
and District Councils"; "The
Election of Parish Councils";
&c., &c.*

Division Lists

*For rapidly and permanently recording the Votes of
Parish Councillors, for or against any Motion.*

SETTLED BY

F. ROWLEY PARKER.

In Books, Price 6s. each.

15.   An 1895 advertisement for a new and
essential guide.

apply to the county council for any of the powers of a parish council to be conferred on a parish meeting. His main point was that the parish meeting (i.e. the 'entire adult inhabitants of every parish') had been given statutory powers by the 1894 Act to restrain its own parish council and even, in some cases, the county council 'from acts of importance'. Isn't it sad, then, that in so many parishes a hundred years later the annual parish meetings are so poorly attended? Surely, as Morrison Davidson encouraged, the aim of the 'denizens of rural England' should be 'to make every adult, male and female, a Parish Councillor, in his own and her own right'.

The Parish Council

The new parish councils were bound to hold an annual general meeting (in addition to the annual parish meeting described earlier) on or within seven days of 15 April at which they would elect a chairman and Overseers. The first chairman, elected in December 1894, could hold office until April 1896 and had the casting vote in questions which were decided by majority voting. As well as this annual meeting, it must hold at least three other meetings during the year and all the meetings were to be open to the public unless the council directed otherwise.

The new parish councils took over most of the non-ecclesiastical powers and duties of the traditional Vestry and many of those of the church-wardens and Overseers, along with the power of the Guardians to sell, exchange or let parish property, the powers (in some instances) of Allotment Managers and those of Burial Boards, where they existed, and of Inspectors for Lighting and Watching, and also of various Commissioners for Baths and Wash-houses, Public Improvements and Public Libraries. It was a grand rationalisation at local level to overcome some of the confusion about who did what on the countless boards and other bodies which had been created during the 19th century. The many pages of the Act, in respect of parish council powers, were boiled down by Morrison Davidson to a lengthy basic list of 41 articles, most of which still apply today.

An alternative and briefer list was printed in the *Sunday Graphic*:

1. Allotments	8. Parish Hall and Offices
2. Cottage Accommodation	9. Recreation Grounds
3. Water Supply	10. Public Lighting
4. Sanitation	11. Public Baths
5. Rights of Way	12. Public Libraries
6. Repair of Footpaths	13. Burial Grounds
7. Preservation of Commons	14. Parish Charities

Local Government Act, 1894.

PARISH COUNCIL.

STATUTORY PROVISIONS CONTROLLING PROCEEDINGS.

It is enacted in the Local Government Act, 1894, in effect, as follows :—

Constitution of Parish Council.

(1.) The Parish Council for a rural parish shall be elected from among the parochial electors of that parish or persons who have during the whole of the twelve months preceding the election resided in the parish, or within three miles thereof, and shall consist of a Chairman and Councillors, and the number of Councillors shall be such as may be fixed from time to time by the County Council, not being less than five nor more than fifteen.

(2.) No person shall be disqualified by sex or marriage for being elected or being a member of a Parish Council.

(3.) The term of office of a Parish Councillor shall be one year.

(4.) On the fifteenth day of April in each year (in this Act referred to as the ordinary day of coming into office of Councillors) the Parish Councillors shall go out of office, and their places shall be filled by newly-elected Councillors.

(5.) The Parish Councillors shall be elected by the parochial electors of the parish.

(6.) The election of Parish Councillors shall, subject to the provisions of this Act, be conducted according to rules framed under this Act for that purpose by the Local Government Board.

(7.) The Parish Council shall in every year, on or within seven days after the ordinary day of coming into office of Councillors, hold an annual meeting.

(8.) At the annual meeting, the Parish Council shall elect, from their own body or from other persons qualified to be Councillors of the parish, a Chairman, who shall, unless he resigns, or ceases to be qualified, or becomes disqualified, continue in office until his successor is elected.

(9.) Every Parish Council shall be a body corporate by the name of the Parish Council, with the addition of the name of the parish, or if there is any doubt as to the latter name, of such name as the County Council after consultation with the Parish Meeting of the parish direct, and shall have perpetual succession, and may hold land for the purposes of their powers and duties without licence in mortmain ; and any act of the Council may be signified by an instrument executed at a meeting of the Council, and under the hands, or, if an instrument under seal is required, under the hands and seals, of the Chairman presiding at the meeting and two other members of the Council.

(10.) With respect to meetings of Parish Councils, the provisions in the First Schedule to this Act shall have effect.—(Section 3.)

16. A reminder about the constitution of the new parish councils, often to be found at the front of the first minute books.

Four Acres and a Cow

It was not the thought of all this street-lighting, public baths or free reading-rooms that excited the majority of the rural population—it was the idea of allotments. And they were not thinking in terms of a small vegetable patch with a row of beans and a few cabbages. Morrison Davidson woke them up to the reality of the new Act about the acreage of land which a parish council could hold and let to villagers. 'The general belief', he said, 'is that it is limited to four acres—three pastoral and one arable—one for each allottee'. Read that again. Four acres *for each allottee*: ample space for a couple of cows and other livestock as well as a very substantial area for growing crops of various kinds.

Today, people may wonder what all the fuss was about: who needs four acres? But anyone who has read the social history books on the subject of, for example, the enclosures, or who has ever tried to be self-sufficient will know exactly why this part of the Parish Councils Act caused such a stir in the countryside.

Cottages

The *Sunday Graphic* felt that the parish council's next most important subject was that of cottage accommodation, although it could do nothing directly to provide better cottages. Its rôle was to report to the district council when any cottage was in an unsanitary condition and it could call upon the district council either to see that the cottage was improved or that better cottages were provided elsewhere. The district had full powers for calling upon owners to put such cottages into repair (at a period, it must be remembered, when some 90 per cent of homes, large and small, were rented rather than owner-occupied) and, if necessary, it could either lease or purchase the cottages itself and repair them, or build new ones. Council housing had been born!

The Adoptive Acts

The five so-called Adoptive Acts were options which only the Parish Meeting could decide upon. They were:

1. Lighting and Watching Act 1833, concerned with the provision of lamps, lamp-posts and lighting material, watch-boxes and fire-engines, all of which could be provided by the parish and paid for out of the rates.
2. Baths and Wash-houses Acts, 1846—82, under which the parish council could build public baths and wash-houses, or create open or covered swimming places, again paid for out of the rates.
3. Burial Acts 1852—85, twelve Acts concerning the provision of burial grounds in the parish.
4. The Public Improvements Act 1860, applying only to parishes with a population of at least 500. The term 'improvements' covered a wide range — for example, the purchase of land by the parish council and the provision of 'public walks', playgrounds, seats, shelters and so on.
5. The Public Libraries Act 1892, under which a parish might provide any or all of: public libraries, public museums, art galleries, science and art schools.

*****

Morrison Davidson concluded his 50 pages of advice with a rallying cry but also with an acute perception of what was likely to happen in reality. He felt that a 'new and better life' was rapidly opening up for the 'Sons of the Soil' to whom his remarks had been addressed and commended them to make the most of it. But he added:

> If I have not patted your 'pastors and masters' on the back, neither have I flattered you. You are what these men of Belial to whom all power has been committed for centuries, have made you. I blame you for nothing: all manhood that could be crushed out of you has been. I shall not even complain if, at the Parish Elections in December, you should disappoint the New Democracy of the towns by showing favour to your old enemies and spurning the advice of your new friends, disinterested as I know it to be. It is not easy to extract the corroding iron of Centuries of *Custom* from the minds of the best of us.

His passions might have been somewhat extreme, but he had foreseen exactly what would happen. The first flaw in this revolution became apparent on that great day in December 1894 when parishes all over the land gathered at their first parish meetings and elected their first parish councils.

Almost without exception, the squire or the parson became chairman of the parish council, and many of its members were the major farmers. In most cases, the existing Assistant Overseer (who, unlike most of the Overseers, received a salary) became clerk to the parish council, providing the continuity with the old Vestry system. Life in the villages hardly changed at all: those who had always run it continued to do so.

East Preston was in the slightly unusual position of having a village population of only 252 but a workhouse population of 162. There was quite a rumpus when the local landowner and churchwarden, Reginald A. Warren, JP, insisted that a parish council was unnecessary as it

17. Members of Bognor Urban District Council, 1897, on the occasion of Queen Victoria's Diamond Jubilee.

would merely increase the rates. Others disagreed and, bravely, a local coastguard stood up and requested a secret ballot 'as he understood there were many persons present who would not dare to openly express an opinion at variance with some Gentlemen present'. One of those gentlemen remarked that Mr. Warren was not the sort of person 'to remember in time to come any independent action on the part of his employees'. In the event, by a public show of hands, there was an overwhelming majority among some 30 electors present who were in favour of a council, and so a parish council they had. But Mr. Warren became its chairman and remained in charge of this village parliament until his death in 1911, having obtained more votes than anyone else in the first ballot. During his chairmanship, the council did almost nothing that would cost any money at all: it was left to the benefactors, such as Warren himself, to provide privately amenities such as recreation grounds and halls.

At **Billingshurst** no fewer than 33 candidates vied for 13 places at the 4 December meeting. The nine members of the first parish council of **Ardingly**, chaired by an MP, were elected from 20 nominations which included the butcher and the baker (but no candlestick-maker), the rector, a builder, a sawyer, a bricklayer, a carpenter, a land agent, a farm bailiff, five farmers, two gentlemen, the secretary and headmaster of Ardingly College and also the village roadman, Caleb Holman (great uncle of one of today's parish councillors, C.H. Izard), described on his nomination paper as 'Labourer' and able to poll 63 votes—top of the poll, with 70, was the village builder. Holman remained on the parish council for 13 years.

The united parishes of **Colgate** and **Lower Beeding** were typical, with the squire and the vicar firmly in place but also a local builder; 11 councillors were elected from a choice of 18 candidates (ten from Lower Beeding, eight from Colgate) by show of hands; and Mr. F. Cripps was elected as Assistant Overseer and Clerk to the Council.

Hurstpierpoint's first chairman was, in effect, the lord of the manor—Mr. W. H. Campion, whose family is still considered in the same light today as they owned the Danny House estate (now a home for 'retired gentlefolk'). **Aldingbourne**'s first meeting was attended by 51 parishioners. **Slindon** elected the squire as its first chairman and the council members included the rector, the headmaster, the estate's agent, the grocer, the landlord of the *Newburgh Arms* and two cottagers. (Ninety years later Slindon's parish council still included a grocer, but the other members were a chief forester, a machine operative, a retired company director, an industrial scientist, a rear admiral, a teacher turned housewife and a hospital sister who was a farmer's wife.)

Bognor elected its first Town Council under the new Act and its fine body of men included a photographer, three solicitors, a town surveyor, two chemists, a brewer, a tea merchant, a schoolmaster and three builders (one of whom, Alfred Adlington, ran the Victoria Theatre from 1897; another was also a house agent and cabinet-maker). At **Poynings** on 4 December eight candidates contested five places and, after a show of hands, two who had gained the same number of votes withdrew; then, after a slightly embarrassing interlude and some consultation among the electors, another withdrew so that the remaining five were duly elected: a farmer, a miller, a labourer and two unspecified; they chose to have their first parish council meeting on the last day of 1894—apparently almost in the dark, as it was not until the following October that they were presented with a large lamp 'from which they were enjoying a good light'.

And so the first parish councils began to settle down to their business.

Chapter 3

Growth and Change

Too soon, that initial enthusiasm mellowed, then waned, faded and all but died—or so it would seem from the story told by countless old minute books. Meetings became routine and poorly attended. The annual parish meeting, which had been trumpeted as the democratic jewel in the local government crown, quickly became an apathetic event which was attended, in the most dire parishes, not even by all the councillors, let alone any of those they represented. In **Washington**, many of the annual parish meetings before the First World War were attended by the chairman—and nobody else at all. The same parish called a formal meeting for 27 December 1900 specifically to consider the 'New Basis or Standard for fair and equal County Rates in the County of West Sussex' and then managed to close the meeting without even mentioning the subject.

The regular council meetings, held in some places every month or two at first, became less and less frequent and sometimes degenerated into annual or at best six-monthly affairs at which the minutes of the last meeting were read and approved, the overseers appointed and that was about it, though sometimes there would be an item on evaluating properties in the parish for rates purposes.

In most parishes, minutes were written to a formula which would say, in too many words, nothing of substance. There is a great deal of procedural formality and the recording of who proposed and seconded what, but very little about details or the thinking and discussion behind proposals and their resolutions. Minutes can be barometers of parish life, but for many years they were so perfunctory that it demands some imagination to know, so to speak, what the weather

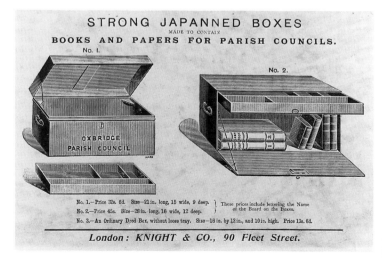

18. An 1895 advertisement encouraging the new parish councils to preserve their records.

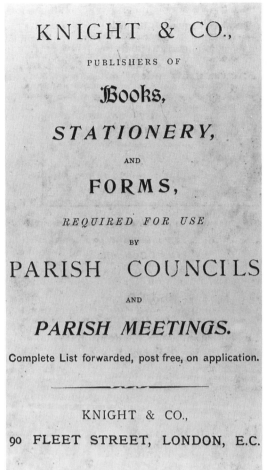

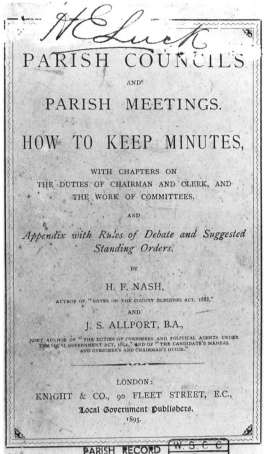

19. An advertisement for stationery, 1895. Paper   20. Parish council chairmen and clerks needed
and parish councils seem to go together.   plenty of basic advice on procedures in 1895.

was really like. From a historical point of view, the background details are much more important
than the formal resolutions, as well as more interesting. We want to know *why*.

Grey though the contents of most minute books were, they were beautifully handwritten in
elegant copperplate which gave them a greater importance than perhaps they merited. And clearly
the greyness was sometimes deceptive. Then, as now, much parish business was carried out in a
far less formal manner: groups and cliques met over a pint or out-of-doors for a gossip and talked
themselves into sorting out problems, or individuals simply *did* something about them without
bothering to have their deeds formally recorded at council meetings. In fact they did what parish
councils and their clerks do best: they were on the ground, aware of day-to-day problems in the
parish and dealing with them on the spot. They only recorded what needed to be formally in writing.

A broad trawl through those minutes usually produces items, even a hundred years ago, that
most parishes still worry about today—above all that hangover from Vestry days: quibbles about
the maintenance of highways and associated traffic problems. Later chapters look at some of
those items in more detail.

****

The first half-century of the parish councils was a time of tremendous change in the countryside and in society in general but it can be hard to trace the threads of those changes through council archives. Yet they are there if the reader persists. Many local changes came about as a result of growth and movement of populations. Table 3 compares parish populations in 1891 and 1991 (the latest census) and, though some are deceptive in that parishes have been combined and boundaries have been altered in intervening years, sometimes the growth is quite startling.

Table 3   Population by parish, 1891 and 1991 (in alphabetical order of parish)

Note: Several parishes which existed in 1891 were 'rationalised' at various stages before 1991—either wholly absorbed into another, or amalgamated where previously divided, or with various boundary adjustments (including into Hampshire and to or from East Sussex). They are not, therefore, directly comparable. 1891 figures are based on those given in *Victoria County History, Sussex*, Vol.2; 1991 figures are based on census profiles published by West Sussex County Council's planning department.

PARISH	1891	1991	PARISH	1891	1991
Albourne	305	580	Clayton	1966	1671
Aldingbourne	798	3202	Climping	248	497
Aldwick		10654	Coates	84	
Alfold (part)	296		Cocking	449	447
Amberley	525	525	Coldwaltham	338	806
Angmering	990	5591	Colgate		697
Appledram	144	165	Compton	264	349
Ardingly	1280	1594	Coombes	86	42
Arundel	2644	3033	Cowfold	945	1781
Ashington	267	1748	Crawley	437	87644
Ashurst	331	253	Cuckfield	5730	2879
Ambersham, North	160		Cuckfield Rural		1667
Ambersham, South	186		Dean, East	303	217
Balcombe	977	1746	Dean, West	611	433
Barlavington	175	137	Didling	61	
Barnham	230	1237	Donnington	191	1695
Beeding, Lower	1284	936	Duncton	259	270
Beeding, Upper	506	3641	Durrington	153	
Bepton	235	262	Earnley	140	392
Bersted, South	849		Eartham	138	96
Bersted		8166	Easebourne	1360	1837
Bignor	159	100	Eastergate	174	3126
Billingshurst	1658	5570	East Grinstead	7569	24383
Binsted	103		Ebernoe		231
Binderton	110		Edburton	359	
Birdham	453	1324	Egdean	75	
Bognor township	4104		Elsted	191	158
Bognor Regis		19836	Felpham	724	9114
Bolney	829	1180	Fernhurst	1020	3064
Bosham	1258	2600	Ferring	226	4148
Botolphs	920		Findon	775	1776
Boxgrove	699	776	Fishbourne		1737
Bramber	169	798	Fishbourne, New	323	
Bramshot (part)	80		Fittleworth	761	916
Broadbridge Heath		3007	Ford	102	1078
Broadwater	15970		Funtington	1020	1432
Burgess Hill		25510	Fulking		271
Burpham	280	194	Goring	561	
Burton	57		Graffham	407	487
Bury	551	668	Greatham	66	
Chidham	241	981	Grinstead, West	1578	2709
Chiltington, West	612	3273	Hardham	124	
Chithurst	277		Harting	1279	1481
Clapham	270	351	Haywards Heath		22624

Heene	1691		Rusper	548	1447
Henfield	2006	4796	Rustington	437	11761
Heyshott	393	337	Selham	101	
Hoathly, West	1442	2188	Selsey	1039	8754
Horsham	10741	22716	Shermanbury	356	530
Horsham, North		17133	Shoreham, New	3393	
Horsted Keynes	932	1485	Shoreham, Old	260	
Houghton	174	93	Shoreham-by-Sea		20638
Hunston	187	1063	Shipley	1061	1115
Hurstpierpoint	2283	5658	Sidlesham	920	1190
Ifield	2817		Singleton	579	459
Iping	457		Slaugham	1616	2192
Itchenor, West	115	474	Slindon	512	534
Itchingfield	492	1455	Slinfold	853	1707
Keymer	3845	5268	Sompting	700	8408
Kingston	431		Southbourne		5988
Kingston-by-Sea	253	622	Southwater		6615
Kirdford	1642	863	Southwick	2564	11087
Lancing	1285	17843	Stedham	558	916
Lavant, East	421	1653	Steyning	1705	5376
Lavington, East		215	Stoke, North		100
Lavington, West		302	Stoke, South	131	56
Linch	111	67	Stoke, West	103	
Linchmere	391	1619	Stopham	151	93
Lindfield	2233		Storrington	1293	3960
Lindfield Rural		2560	Stoughton	618	741
Lindfield Urban		5628	Sullington	320	2177
Littlehampton	4455	23301	Sutton	325	226
Lodsworth	592	645	Tangmere	164	1693
Loxwood		1406	Tarring, West	1035	
Lurgashall	768	633	Terwick	168	
Lyminster	1693	360	Thakeham	494	1755
Madehurst	176	132	Tillington	871	534
Marden		62	Thorney, West	150	898
Marden, East	64		The Gumber	27	
Marden, North	39		Tortington	288	
Merston	108		Treyford	114	96
Middleton	40		Trotton	539	313
Middleton-on-Sea		4299	Turners Hill		1534
Midhurst	1674	4614	Twineham	314	295
Mid Lavant	366		Up Marden	310	
Milland		981	Up Waltham	67	24
Mundham, North	373	1134	Walberton	665	1926
Newtimber	203	75	Warminghurst	70	
Nuthurst	814	1688	Warnham	1060	1719
Northchapel	742	714	Warningcamp	159	174
Oving	1973	775	Washington	831	1035
Pagham	887	4899	Westbourne	2409	2054
Parham	58	185	Westhampnett	505	416
Patching	270	230	Wiggonholt	52	
Petworth	2867	2921	Wisborough Green	1599	1367
Plaistow		1772	Wiston	311	216
Poling	196	168	Wittering, East	214	3431
Poynings	305	284	Wittering, West	582	2750
Preston, East	417	5338	Woodmancote	314	460
Pulborough	1787	6309	Woolavington	505	
Pyecombe	353	207	Woolbeding	390	178
Rackham Hamlet	134		Worth	4047	9714
Racton	100		Yapton	629	3454
Rogate	953	1472			
Rudgwick	1177	2324	Chichester City	7890	23258
Rumboldswyke	1497				

Life jogged along for the parish councils, marked by perhaps four major jolt-points along the way: two world wars and two local government reviews. In between, there were jubilees and coronations, and the parish council was a natural body to co-ordinate local celebrations, usually setting up a committee of some kind to do so. Queen Victoria's death after such a long reign went unremarked by most parishes, though her jubilee had been celebrated in a material way by

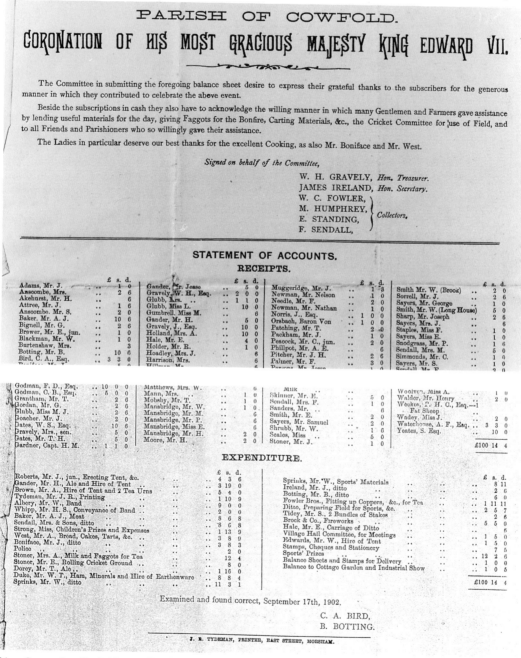

21. Coronation festivities at Cowfold, 1902. Donations by a long list of subscribers ranged from threepence to £10.

No. 157

Twineham Coronation Festivities.

aug 9th 1902.
JUNE 27th, 1902.

Long Live the King.

Service at Parish Church 2 p.m.   Sports 3 p.m.
Children's Tea 4.30 p.m.   Knife & Fork Tea 5.30 p.m.
Bonfire 10 p.m.

Admit _____

No.157   Knife & Fork Tea 5.30 p.m.

22.   Coronation festivities at Twineham, 1902.

some. **Angmering**, for example, had opened a parish reading room and **Northchapel** dedicated a stained-glass window in the church in 1897 and held a children's tea party to the music of a band. Many a parish celebrated the coronation of Edward VII in 1902 and **Cowfold** made a tremendous day of it, as the poster shows.

Twineham celebrated it too, and they formed another coronation committee in 1937, spending the balance of their fund-raising (9s. 6d.) on a copper beech tree for the school grounds. The tiny and fragmented parish of **Bepton** (which had defeated a motion to become a parish council in 1894 and remained a parish meeting until its electors numbered 201 in 1970) had a programme of festivities for the coronation of George V in 1911 and also formed coronation committees in 1937 and 1953. **Aldingbourne** had celebrated the 1911 coronation on 22 June with a church service followed by 'entertainment by the school children' in the meadow opposite the Forge, then a 'good meat tea' with alcohol and minerals for the adults and a 'plain tea' for the children before a 'capital' programme of sports and a firework display in the evening, rounded off with a chorus of 'God Save the King'.

In 1935 **Lavant** parish council arranged for local celebrations of the Royal Silver Jubilee by putting an extra penny on the rates to pay for a children's tea, an evening social for the adults, and jubilee mugs for the children.

Wars

The 'Great War' broke out before the parish councils had reached their coming-of-age. It must have made a huge impact on every village in the land with so many men leaving their families (and perhaps their local area for the first time in their lives) and so many never coming home again. But the war is hardly mentioned in parish council minutes. The same councillors and chairmen, so often of the older generation anyway, simply carried on with the usual mundane business of appointing overseers and questioning rates valuations. **Washington** gave up altogether and held no parish meetings at all during the 1914-18 war. **Poynings**' minutes mentioned the word 'war' for the first time on 18 February 1916, when a letter about the War Food Society was referred to the Flower Show committee; at the same meeting the clerk's claim for exemption from military service was supported unanimously as he was considered to be 'indispensible to the Parish', and his claim continued to be supported at three further meetings (even after an appeal), though in November 1917 the council resolved that, if he was to be called up after all, his wife would take his place as clerk. The parish council tried equally hard to ignore the second world war, even though the Battle of Britain was fought in the skies above Poynings and Bomber Command assembled its Lancasters over the Downs. Later this thrifty council (which secured £6 from 'the military' for damage to a footpath) ensured that victory celebrations were funded by private contributions rather than from parish council sources, and when a guinea was sent to the Royal Sussex Memorial Fund the auditor disallowed it, so that each councillor had to fork out three shillings in repayment.

YOUR KING AND COUNTRY THANK YOU.
HOME WORDS No. 168
Christmas Greetings from your friends at Westbourne

23.   Christmas postcard sent from Westbourne during the First World War.

Twineham, like other parishes in the county, received a letter from the county council in March 1918 'inviting an application for a lecturer on Fruit Preserving' but it was resolved to take no action 'owing to the smallness of the Parish and the small quantity of fruit grown'. Another small parish, **Chithurst**, had exactly the same reaction to the horticultural society of the West Sussex Agricultural Executive committee: it simply did not have any surplus fruit and vegetables for marketing, as that group had suggested. Chithurst did manage to collect £6 1s. 0d. for the National Relief Fund but decided it was too small a community to set up a parish committee to deal with unemployment distress, as suggested by the local Distress Committee in Midhurst. It was also a bit put out at being told in a circular how to farm: 'The farmers of the parish', it stated in dudgeon, 'have done, are doing, and will continue to do their best to farm the land in the most suitable manner'. That was in 1915. The following year the county council's War Agriculture committee sent another circular to its parishes on the subject of 'Rats and Sparrows', in response to which Chithurst's parish meeting resolved: 'Considering the geographical configuration of the Parish of Chithurst and the neighbouring parishes, the problem ... should be dealt with by the District Council'. There was a bounty on rats' tails at the time.

Amberley, in 1914, was among those who considered approaches from the Prince of Wales' National Relief Fund and the county Distress Committee. **Bersted** decided to co-opt one of its electors on to the latter but thereafter the committee was never mentioned again. However, councillors put together a list of those electors who were serving at the front so that they could be sent a weekly dispatch—presumably of parish news. Otherwise, like all the other parishes, they simply continued to discuss routine matters such as blocked watercourses, footpaths and so on during the war, but the meetings, which had already dwindled from monthly (in 1895) to quarterly by 1915, had very little business and the minutes were written in several different hands.

24. Mr. Stent and his fine Large Black of the Sussex type at Cocking Causeway. Many cottagers kept a pig.

Lavant responded to the 'desire of many local residents' in 1917 to form pig clubs and the clerk wrote to Lady March asking for tenants to be provided with materials to make pig pens and for ideas of appropriate rules for a pig club.

For several years after the Great War, there was an old German field gun outside St Mary's Church, **Slaugham**. A parish council meeting in August 1929 received a letter from several ex-servicemen asking why the gun had been removed and on whose authority. 'They honoured the gun and wondered why it was removed. Soon after its removal the Union Jack was flown, and while they honoured the flag they also honoured the Gun, having fought in the war for both.' The chairman said it was removed by the authority of those who had put it there in the first place—the Rector and the churchwardens. Apparently the Royal Sussex regiment had a number of guns for disposal at the end of the war in 1918 and the rector of the time 'thought it would be nice to have a gun outside the church'. By 1929 it was in a state of disrepair: the wheels were falling off and 'once it had been pushed down the hill with the intention of being run into the pond but it never got there. Obviously the only thing to do was to remove a derelict object'.

Many a parish was instrumental in the installation of local memorials to the war dead, be it a stone cross by the roadside or on the green, a tablet in the church, a recreation ground, a reading room or a memorial hall; some of these were built after the first war, others after the second, and they are described in the next chapter.

By the time of that second war, several parishes at last had their first women members on the council—a situation which, in theory, could have occurred right from the start and which in practice was often the first step in a woman's political career. **Bersted** had three women by then, and a woman was elected to the chair in 1942. **Pulborough**'s first women had been elected to its parish council just after the first war. **Keymer** voted in its first woman to the parish council in 1922.

The Second World War, in reality, had a much greater direct effect in the villages than had the first—especially from an influx of evacuees and, in some areas, large encampments or movements of troops, quite apart from the drama of bombers and dogfights, and the lesser drama of rationing and blackouts. But there were no eloquent rallying calls for the parish to help the war effort, no patriotic gestures—at least, not in the minutes, regardless of what really went on in the parishes. However, this second war woke them up and there was a genuine revival of interest in parish councils after the war. Whereas before, elections were hardly able to raise

25.   Dedication of Eastergate War Memorial, 1920, by the Duke of Richmond. William Collins (chairman of the parish council) is on the right.

26.   The influx of evacuees. London schoolchildren arriving at Billingshurst, 1939.

enough candidates for a quorum in some places, the first post-war elections saw a rash of candidates in many parishes—there were 29 candidates for **Pulborough** parish council's 13 seats at the annual parish meeting in March 1946.

It was after the Second World War that a Labour government created the welfare state which, in effect, forever removed from the parishes one of the core rôles that had been theirs for centuries: the tradition of caring for their own poor, aged and otherwise weaker parishioners. In fact they had long since lost that rôle: even their nominal involvement by appointing Overseers had come to an end in 1927. The district councils had taken over most of the parish's 'caring' rôles when the Vestry meetings became parish councils and parish meetings.

Local Government Reviews

It took more than wars to wake up some of the parish councils. They were far more alert to another threat a decade after the first war had ended: a new Local Government Bill, which became an Act in 1929. This affected them directly in that it led to a review of their boundaries— something which central government seems to be unable to keep its hands off for long. There have been many tinkerings with local council boundaries over the years and they are at it again even now. Parishes had found themselves being shuffled like packs of cards for a fresh deal in 1835 and 1869. Then in 1889, when the county councils were formed, another shuffle of boundaries had been made 'as to arrange that no Union, borough, sanitary district, or parish shall be situate in more than one county' and so on. Bits of east and west Sussex had changed from one to the other; parishes were moved into different Unions either wholly or in part, and one or two even changed county. Map 2 gives some idea of what was going on.

In 1933 West Sussex County Council sent every one of its parishes a detailed document describing exactly which bits of what it proposed to change. Map 3 shows its intentions, and it gave various reasons for its proposals. For example, it wanted to reduce the Rural Districts from eight to six for 'more efficient and effective county and local administration': **Westbourne** and **Westhampnett** rural districts would be combined and called **Chichester** Rural District; **Thakeham** and **Steyning West** rural districts would be combined and called **Chanctonbury** Rural District; **East Preston** rural district would be renamed **Worthing** Rural District and its boundaries adjusted; **Horsham**, **Midhurst** and **Petworth** rural districts remained intact. There were three urban districts—**Bognor Regis**, **Littlehampton** and **Shoreham-by-Sea**. Finally there was the Municipal Borough of **Worthing**, and the City of **Chichester** (which would absorb all of **New Fishbourne** and part of **Donnington**).

The county council also wanted to rationalise the parishes themselves: it intended to sort out the remaining nonsense of 'detached' or divided parishes—little islands floating in the middle of nowhere which it decided to stick on to 'the most appropriate parish'. And it wanted to unite several parishes 'which either by reason of their small size or population do not justify the continuance of their existence as separate parishes', after which proper parish councils could be constituted in the enlarged parishes of, specifically, **Ashington**, **Bramber**, **Parham**, **Compton** and **Middleton**. There were other adjustments 'to overcome the inconvenience of existing boundaries'. The document gave detailed tables for every parish in the county including its population and acreage in 1931 (and by extrapolation its population density), its rateable value, the penny rate and the rates levied, and the number of parish councillors appropriate to the size of the parish.

Suddenly a lot of parishes were faced with the threat of disappearance into another parish and not all of them welcomed the prospect. For centuries there have been rivalries between neighbouring villages, sometimes friendly but sometimes quite aggressive. It was the map-of-Africa syndrome, whereby a greater power decreed boundary changes for the sake of its own convenience without always taking into account what might be called cultural differences.

The proposals for united parishes were (with the name of the combined parish in brackets):

Binsted and **Tortington** (Binsted)
Ifield with part of **Crawley** (Crawley)
Graffham and **Selham** (Graffham)
Treyford and **Didling** (Treyford)
Fittleworth and **Coates** (Fittleworth)
Egdean and **Petworth** (Egdean)
Bramber and **Buttulphs** [*sic*] (Bramber)
Upper Beeding and **Edburton** (Upper Beeding)
Lancing and **Coombes** (Lancing)
Amberley and **North Stoke** (Amberley)
Coldwaltham and **Hardham** (Coldwaltham)
Parham and **Greatham** and **Rackham** (Parham)
West Dean and **Binderton** (West Dean)
Oving and **Merston** (Oving)
West Stoke and **Funtington** (Funtington)
Compton and **Up Marden** (Compton)
East Marden and **North Marden** (Marden)
Stoughton and **Racton** (Stougton)
Westbourne and **Thorney** (Westbourne)

They did not all give in without a fight. The *Southern Weekly News* headlined an article on 22 May 1937: 'BINSTED IS ON STRIKE!'. The people of Binsted had been waging a war against the county council during the four intervening years to keep themselves separate from Tortington, three miles away. Binsted simply refused to acknowledge the change thrust upon it and 'ignored sleepy-eyed Tortington even more than Tortington ignores Binsted. Binsted people will not walk to Tortington for a Parish meeting. Tortington will not come to Binsted. Attempts made to hold a meeting on neutral ground have failed because both sides, by mutual consent, adjourn the meeting almost before it begins, and make no decisions.'

Binsted's rector, the Rev. William Drury, and a local farmer, Mr. S. H. Upton, informed the reporter that this was 'a strike to the bitter end'. 'Slowly our identity is going', declared the rector. 'Fancy asking our people to walk three miles to a parish meeting! It is impossible to work with Tortington. It is a matter I am very hot about. The trouble is that the Rural District Councils are antediluvian, useless. We used to enjoy our parish meetings so much, too. We could all meet and see each other and talk over matters. Now all that is lost.'

Farmer and donkey-breeder Upton was equally adamant. 'Binsted does not want Tortington and Tortington does not want Binsted. There's the whole problem. Binsted and Tortington have no common interests. Take the Coronation: Binsted had its own show, a great show. We had a grand time. But Tortington did nothing at all. They went in with Arundel and enjoyed their celebrations. You see, Tortington is like Arundel. It is owned by the Duke of Norfolk and the people are tenants, while we in Binsted have our own farms and holdings and we are proud of our inheritance. We strongly object to being taken over like this; we refuse to be obliterated.'

As the present clerk of Walberton parish council puts it, Binsted typifies the attitude of 'Sussex won't be druv'! In the end, they joined with Walberton in 1943 and, ironically, Tortington was broken up a few years ago to be split between Walberton and Arundel.

The post-war rekindling of enthusiasm found substance when the Sussex Association of Local Councils was set up in 1947, covering both East and West Sussex, with the aims and objects of taking 'all such steps as may be necessary or desirable in the interests of parishes in the area'

LOCAL GOVERNMENT BOUNDARIES COMMISSION.

DIAGRAM

of the

ALTERATIONS PROPOSED

By the Boundaries Commission,

In the COUNTY of

SUSSEX (EAST AND WEST)

Showing

CIVIL PARISHES ADDED TO THE COUNTY	- - - Hatched Red	
CIVIL PARISHES TRANSFERRED FROM THE COUNTY	- Hatched Green	
OLD COUNTY BOUNDARY	- - - Thus - - -	
NEW COUNTY BOUNDARY	- - - Shown in thick Red band	
UNION BOUNDARIES RETAINED	- - - Shown in thin Red line	
UNION BOUNDARY ABOLISHED	- - - Shown thus, in Black	
NEW UNION BOUNDARY	- - - Shown thus, in Red	
URBAN SANITARY DISTRICTS	- - - Coloured Grey	

Scale of this Diagram 4 Miles to 1 Inch.

References

Towns with over 100,000 Inhabitants	
Towns with over 50,000 Inhabitants	
Towns with less than 50,000 Inhabitants	
Workhouses	
Villages	
County Boundary	
Parish Boundary	
Railways	
Abutting Counties	

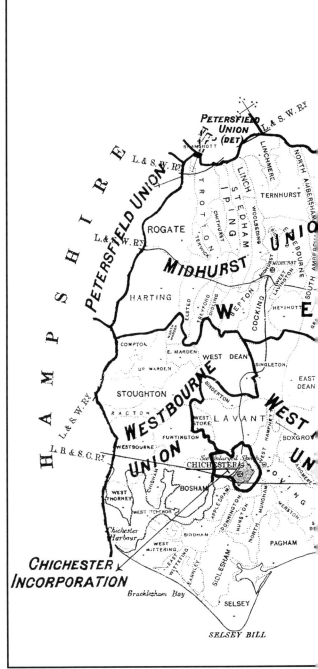

2. West and part of East Sussex: proposed parish and union boundaries, 1888.

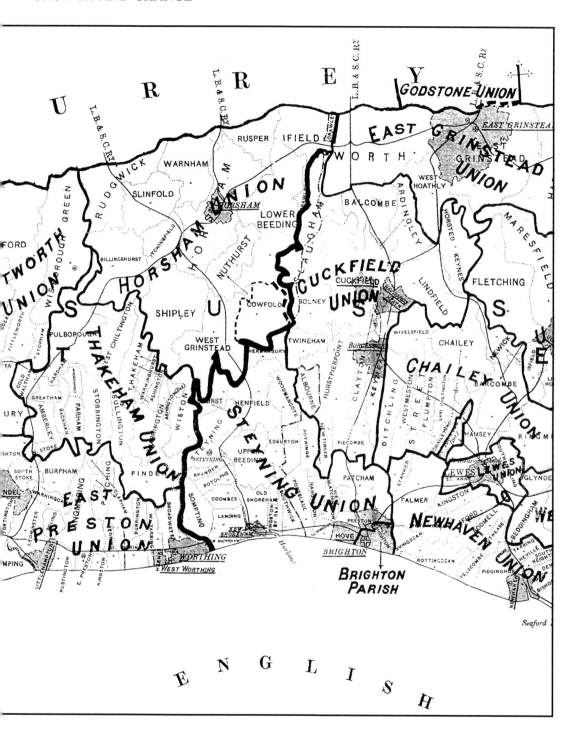

WEST SUSSEX

LOCAL GOVERNMENT ACT 1929.

SECTION 46.

FIRST GENERAL REVIEW OF COUNTY DISTRICTS

DIAGRAM MAP

Scale 2

3. West Sussex: proposed boundary changes, 1929.

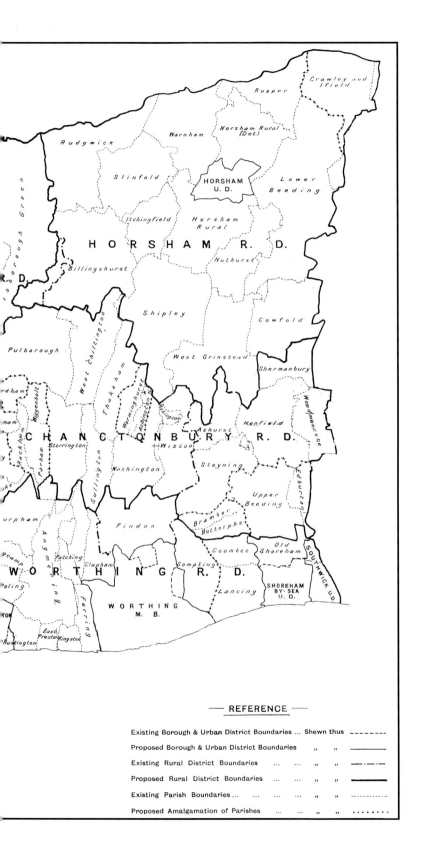

to protect and promote its members' interests, to assist them in performing their duties and in developing the social, cultural and recreational life of parishes and villages and, in general, to promote good local government. It had come too late for some, and was unable to save a few others.

Chithurst, which opted to become a parish council instead of a parish meeting from 1946, was constantly threatened with disappearance in its own right. In 1953 Midhurst RDC proposed to reduce its 26 parishes to a mere 16, which meant *inter alia* the breaking up of Chithurst (the suggestion from Midhurst was that a new parish of Milland should be created, and Chithurst should be transferred partly into Milland and partly into Trotton). This scheme was abandoned 'indefinitely' in 1954, to the relief of the ten threatened parishes, but was mentioned again in 1956-7. Nothing happened, but in 1962 there was yet another threat to create Milland and absorb Chithurst. Again, it didn't happen and the little parish council continued to meet in its small hall in Borden Wood Village, but it could not fight for ever. In 1970, at the invitation of **Stedham** parish council, there was a special meeting of local parishes (Iping, Stedham, Chithurst, Trotton, Linch and Woolbeding) to review their boundaries as requested by the county council. These were the old long, narrow parishes—anathema to map-makers—and at that meeting on 14 December 1970 Chithurst gave in to the inevitable: it agreed to lose its separate identity and to be merged with the parishes of Iping and Trotton. What was once the Domesday parish of Titeherste, worth 100 eels in 1086, had been felled. In the event, in 1972 it was taken partly into a newly combined parish of Trotton-with-Chithurst and partly into the brand new parish of **Milland**, which was finally born in April 1972. The last meeting of Chithurst parish council and its last annual parish meeting were held in March 1972: no members of the public bothered to attend, and only three councillors. Neighbouring **Iping** found itself divided up as well: part went into a new combined parish of Stedham-with-Iping and part into Milland. But valiant little **Linch** defied them all and remained resolutely itself (as a parish meeting), as did **Woolbeding**.

That was the year of the second big local government shake-up in which county boundaries as well as parish boundaries were on the move. This time the mid-Sussex parishes found themselves yet again being pulled from one county to another. There had been a lot of to-ing and fro-ing in the years immediately preceding the Local Government Act 1972 and, as Charles Arnold Baker remarked in his book *Local Council Administration* (3rd edn. 1989): '... little government time or civil service talent could be spared for the increasingly exasperating but admittedly small-scale problems of the parishes'. A Labour government set up what came to be known as the Redcliffe-Maude Royal Commission on Local Government, which published its report in 1969 proposing a two-tier system 'in which the major or unitary authority wielded all the defined statutory powers possessed hitherto by council, borough and district councils, and in which the minor, or local council was empowered on a parochial scale to do what it pleased for its people'. What excitement in the parishes! Power to the parish? Well, no: although the government accepted the report, it promptly lost the election in June 1970. The 63,000 parish councillors in England and Wales were crestfallen. They had been operating in impossible conditions for years. As Arnold Baker puts it: 'The principle feature of parish administration until that date was the straight waistcoat of controls under which it had to operate' and which thoroughly discouraged the exercise of initiative and enterprise at parish council level, drowning the councillors in a pettyfogging sea of technicalities and burying them under a mountain of formalities for every simple idea. Parish councils were prevented *by law* 'from acting on the promptings of foresight normal in private and business life'.

The new Conservative government decided that local government did indeed need a thorough reform and drew up a short, simple White paper based on a two-tier system and recognising that the parish councils were vital as the more intimate local representation in rural areas. But what about the urban ones? What about the boroughs and urban districts which would lose their separate identity in a two-tier system?

After the Local Government Act 1972 came into effect on 1 April 1974, the old distinction between urban and rural parishes disappeared: they were all just parishes. Urban boroughs and urban districts were abolished; rural boroughs became parishes, and the old rural parishes remained parishes. If a parish had no parish council, its district council must create one if the parish had 200 or more electors, or if the parish had 151—199 electors and its parish meeting resolved to have a parish council. If there were 150 or fewer electors, there was some discretion as to whether a parish council could be created. The previous boroughs and urban districts could become parishes; and almost any English parish could resolve to have a town council, in which case its area would be called a town.

The 1972 Act was the one that played about with the counties, creating new ones through mergers and boundary changes, and shrinking some of the remaining ones by hiving off some of their territory to new metropolitan authorities. The main effect in West Sussex was that its boundary with East Sussex was shifted a considerable distance eastwards, as Map 4 shows: it gained a chunk of new parishes and an extra 125,000 people. But its 16 main councils were reduced to eight: the county council itself and only seven district councils (Adur, Arun, Chichester, Crawley, Horsham, Mid-Sussex and Worthing). There were five 'successor' councils to succeed former borough or urban district councils, with the same powers as parish councils—**Arundel**, **Chichester**, **Littlehampton**, **Burgess Hill** and **East Grinstead**. Several of the newly acquired parishes from the east had been switched across the border in the past and were beginning to feel a little disorientated, leaping back and forth over the boundary like schoolgirls over a skipping-rope.

The idea of town councils appealed to some, though the only real difference from a parish council was that you could have a mayor. **Bognor Regis**, which had been an urban district council since the 1890s (whisper it not that it was originally part of South Bersted parish until the Bognor Local Board was created in 1866), became a town council in 1985. **Midhurst**, which had been an ancient manorial borough and had boasted a town hall and town crier in the 19th century, lost its borough status in 1883; it became a rural district council in due course and had a hankering to make itself an urban district in 1903, but the local parishes objected strongly, saying that it would be to the detriment of the rural district as a whole and the outer parts of it in particular as Midhurst would grab all the best bits for itself. It lost its rural district status anyway as a result of the 1972 Act and it became a town council. **Steyning** thought long and hard about whether it was a village or a town and took a vote on the subject in 1987 when it decided, by a majority of three, to remain a parish though its chairman wanted it to be a town council as its population had by then risen to 6,000.

Rustington briefly became a township: its lively and growing community felt it deserved a strong and effective council and that some external bodies had policies which did not include consultation with mere parish councils but did include town councils of similar size. By then Rustington had more than three dozen factories, some 130 shops, four banks, three pubs and 12 building societies to serve a population of over 13,500—quite substantial for a parish. In 1989 Rustington's parish council resolved that the parish should have the status of a town, and the chairman and vice chairman of the council became respectively the town's mayor and deputy mayor. But it didn't last any longer than 200 days: the local populace didn't like being a town, they wanted to remain as a village and a public meeting was called in February 1990. The hall was filled with 210 people, 203 of whom voted against the village becoming a town. At the next council meeting, after a second vote, a motion was carried by six votes to five and Rustington reverted to having a parish council again. That is exactly what parish meetings are for: to counter the parish council.

Haywards Heath became a town council in 1987, having been a neighbourhood council for a couple of years while it awaited a Whitehall decision after a referendum in March 1984 showed that 75 per cent of its voters were in favour of a town council rather than a parish council.

4. Sussex: the ancient parishes and the pre- and post- 1974 boundary between East and West Sussex.

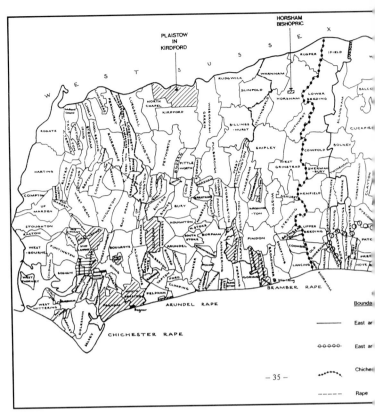

5. Parishes of West Sussex, with electoral divisions as at 1994.

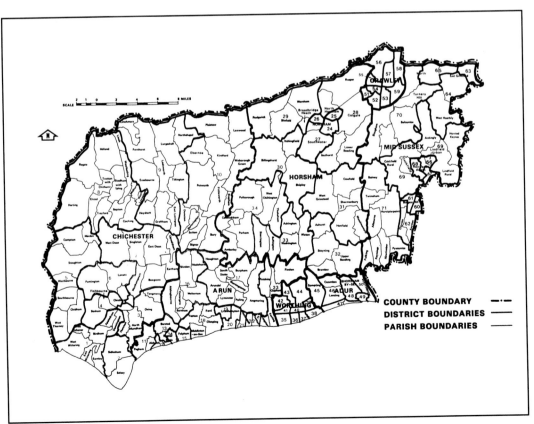

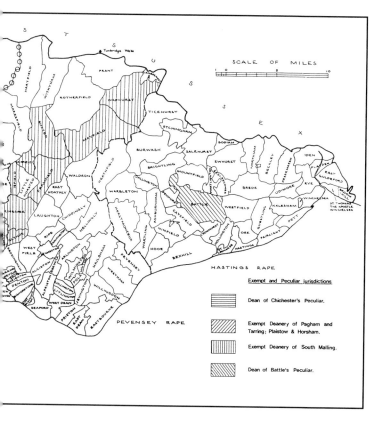

KEY TO ELECTORAL DIVISIONS

CHICHESTER

1. The Witterings
2. Selsey and Sidlesham
3. Chichester South
4. Chichester West
5. Bourne
6. Chichester South
7. Chichester East
8. Midhurst
9. Fernhurst
10. Petworth

ARUN

11. Nyetimber
12. Bognor Regis
13. Bersted
14. Hotham
15. Felpham
16. Fontwell
17. Arundel and Angmering
18. Middleton
19. Littlehampton North
20. Littlehampton Town
21. Rustington West
22. Preston Manor
23. Arun East

HORSHAM

24. Riverside
25. Roffey
26. Hurst
27. Southwater
28. Holbrook
29. Warnham
30. Billingshurst
31. Henfield
32. Steyning
33. Storrington
34. Pulborough

WORTHING

35. Goring-by-Sea
36. West Parade
37. Richmond
38. East Worthing
39. Broadwater
40. West Tarring
41. Maybridge
42. Durrington
43. Salvington
44. Cissbury

ADUR

45. Sompting
46. Lancing
47. Saltings
48. Shoreham
49. Kingston Buci
50. Southwick

CRAWLEY

51. Bewbush
52. Broadfield
53. Tilgate
54. Gossops Green
55. Ifield
56. Langley Green
57. Northgate Three Bridges
58. Pound Hill
59. Furnace Green

MID SUSSEX

60. Burgess Hill East
61. Burgess Hill Central
62. Hassocks and Burgess Hill West
63. East Grinstead East
64. East Gringstead South
65. Imberdown
66. Lindfield
67. Haywards Heath East
68. Haywards Heath West
69. Cuckfield Rural
70. Mid Sussex North
71. Mid Sussex South

Another neighbourhood council had changed its status in April 1986, when Mid-Sussex found itself with two new parishes: **Cuckfield** parish council took over from its 11-year-old neighbourhood council; and **Turners Hill** was carved out of the parish of Worth.

Then there was **Chichester** itself, an ancient city which suffered the indignity of demotion to a mere parish in 1974. That meant it also lost the right to grant 'Freedoms'. But a new Local Government Bill in 1980 gave the local MP a chance to slip in an amendment allowing Chichester and six ancient Royal Boroughs to reclaim their ancient rights. Chichester promptly bestowed the Freedom of their City to the Military Police Corps, which had moved to Roussillon Barracks from Woking in 1964.

So it was that the parishes weathered the storms of reorganisation from on high, their enthusiasm waxing and waning as the graph continued to oscillate. It slipped into another of its troughs with many changes, but in the last four or five years there has been a marked change in attitude and the parish councils of West Sussex are waking up again, as Chapter 7 will show. No doubt many have been encouraged by the words of the present Secretary of State for the Environment, John Gummer, who declared during a radio interview in September 1993 that 'town and parish councils should have as much delegated power as possible, because they are nearest to the people'. [*Today* programme, BBC Radio 4, 30 September 1993.] West Sussex's parish councils are watching with interest the current review of local government.

Chapter 4

Nitty Gritty

What, then, have the parish councils actually been doing for all those decades since their birth in 1894? Actually, quite a lot, especially in their enthusiastic phases (at the beginning, after each of the world wars, and today). Some of the major themes were inherited from the busy Vestry meetings and continue today, in particular highways (and traffic), housing, rights of way and open spaces. Involvement in the consideration of planning applications was a much later and now rapidly growing concern of the parishes.

Nuthurst, a rural parish to the south-east of Horsham, is fairly typical. In the early days, in an age when travel could be quite difficult, the attendance at meetings was as thin as the minuting of them. The first Minute Book was in use for nearly 60 years; the second volume, as impressively bound as the first, covered only 19 years; the third, no longer leather, a mere 10 years. The minutes were handwritten until 1974, after which they were typed and the pages stuck into the bound book—a laborious process which many a clerk will recognise. Today Nuthurst uses a looseleaf ring binder instead. (**Poynings** was more advanced: its parish council had a typewriter back in 1961, and its present clerk remarks: 'The torrent of documents emanating from higher tiers of local government continues to grow but at least the Clerk no longer has to copy out in copperplate every letter received and despatched.')

Most of Nuthurst's councillors of old seemed to stay on the council for many years, often until death—and the frequency of the latter apparently prompted a resolution for the clerk to send off a wreath as soon as he knew that a member had died, without waiting for further authority from his council. There have been only seven chairmen (including the current one) over the hundred years, two of them dying in office, and only seven clerks (including the current one) of whom also two died in office.

Many of the issues recorded in the old minutes are still on the agenda today—Nuthurst is still struggling with public footpaths, unsafe bridges, overgrown hedges, the dumping of rubbish, flooded roads, vandalism and badly parked vehicles. It is also still concerned about affordable housing, a problem which first arose in 1919 when the council was asked whether there was a shortage of houses for the working classes. This issue was referred to as 'workmen's cottages' in the 1920s and 1930s; then it became 'council cottages' and, in the 1950s, 'council houses'. In the late 1950s Nuthurst parish council was trying to get housing for 'labouring and artisan class tenants'—and this turned out to be the parish council's first real involvement with planning matters, a subject of major activity today. In the 1990s it is still pressing for affordable houses for local people and 'social housing'.

Roads were always on the agenda in one form or another, and as far back as 1925 Nuthurst parish council was asked to support a 'London and South Coast Motorway' to Brighton. Well, the motorway to Brighton has yet to be completed ...

27. New council houses at Petworth, 1930,
built by the Boxalls of Tillington.

THE LONDON-BRIGHTON MOTORWAY

A Special Road

for

Motor Vehicles Only

☐ LONDON
○ TOLWORTH
ASHTEAD ○   ○ EPSOM
DORKING ○   ○ ○ REDHILL
               REIGATE
NEWDIGATE ○
HORSHAM ○
           ○ COWFOLD
           ○ PYECOMBE
HOVE ☐ BRIGHTON

MOTOR ROADS DEVELOPMENT SYNDICATE LIMITED
34, Broadway Court, Broadway, Westminster, S.W.1.

28. Prospectus for the country's first proposed
motorway, c.1925.

Pulborough's first annual parish meeting, on 25 March 1895 at the Pulborough School Room, was called to consider the expediency of adopting the Lighting Act, a subject which became the main concern of the new parish council's 13 members for several years. Next they turned their attention to water supplies and called a special meeting on the subject in 1910, which agreed that there should be a water supply for Pulborough and that the parish should discuss with **Storrington** the possibility of a joint scheme.

In 1924 there was a minute asking if steps could be taken for the provision of a scavenging cart, which was badly needed in the parish. Nothing happened, and the same subject was raised seven years later, in 1931. Two years on, Pulborough parish council unanimously agreed to a trial voluntary collection of rubbish by an individual who was prepared to collect household refuse from those who wished at a reasonable charge to be mutually agreed.

By the 1940s Pulborough's parish council had widened the scope of its business to talk about recreation fields, car-parking and footpaths but perhaps it lacked the flavour of the old Vestry days, the minutes and account books of which give so much more of an insight into the daily lives and concerns of the parish's inhabitants. It is so much easier to identify with individuals like James Burchell who, it was minuted in 1801, 'wants a hog fattening' and Robert Blunden who 'wants present relief and a Nurse for wife (ill)', and Benjamin Netley who 'wants Cloathes for Girl going to service' and William Joyes who wanted a 'Round frock for himself' (refused) whereas William Slater was granted '1 bedgown and 1 pettecoat for Girls', though he had asked for two of each. Then there were the expenses paid in 1745 'for a Warrant for John Brooks and Daniel Howard, expenses for Carry him to the Cunstable; expenses to have Will Standen Examined but Could Not Get it dun'. And how about 'Paid for a Mountebanks Packet for ye Widow Brockhurst'? (A Mountebanks Packet was apparently a little parcel of quack medicines sold by cheapjacks at local fairs.) Why has all the colour been drained from parish life as recorded in the minute books of parish councils?

Fire!

Parishes in the Vestry days and often as parish councils were responsible for their own fire-fighting. Some had basic fire-fighting equipment of their own or even their own fire-engine, probably pulled by a team of men or, if to hand, a horse or two. The archives of **Angmering**'s parish council, for example, contain papers relating to its fire brigade up to 1955; **Steyning** had a fire brigade committee in the 1920s and 1930s; **Storrington**'s Vestry meeting was discussing a scheme in 1885 to obtain a 'fire engine, ladder or escape'; **Hurstpierpoint** had its own fire

29. Henfield Fire Brigade, 1908, with two callboys in the background.

engine. **Henfield** had a splendid fire brigade (photographed here in 1908). Henfield's system was probably typical: each voluntary fireman's house was indicated by a sign and there was a gang of 'callboys' whose job it was to run at top speed to each of those houses and summon the men in case of fire. Henfield parish council had started its fire brigade in 1904, with a handcart as its fire-fighting appliance until one of the parish councillors presented the brigade with a horse-drawn manual fire-engine in 1906—its first outing was to a big fire at Cowfold Lodge. The engine continued to be used until 1934, when the parish council took out a loan of £300 from the county council to buy a 1915 Dennis model fire-engine and sold the old horse-drawn one for £2. The parish council continued to run its own fire brigade until the unit was taken over by the county council. Henfield also had its own one-man ambulance, made in 1884 and purchased by the parish council in 1908. It was kept at the fire station and was still in use in the village in the 1930s—it is now in Henfield parish council's museum.

Water

Water, more closely linked with sanitation than with fire-fighting, had been the concern of the old Vestry for a long time and continued to be a problem for some of the parish councils in one way or another. In 1907, **Twineham** parish council formally minuted the fact that they 'quite realised the advisability of having a proper Water Supply in the Parish providing the cost is not too great'. In 1909 the water company had agreed to supply water in bulk at 1s. 6d. per thousand gallons and the parish council hoped that the RDC would take the necessary steps to supply the parish with water 'providing the initial costs do not exceed £1,300'.

In 1906 the parish of **Northchapel** experienced a drought from 5 June to 2 October, which inspired the setting up of a parish council committee to survey all the parish's water sources. They found 120 of them—springs, wells, ponds and tanks, some of which still had a plentiful supply though several cottages had no water supply at all, drought or no drought. They concluded that Blackdown was the parish's main source of water.

Other parishes suffered more often from flooding than from drought, especially those near the rivers. **Balcombe** suffered the destruction of a road and bridge in 1880 because sluices were in a state of disrepair, and the subject of bridges was frequently on its Vestry agenda. Riverside parishes such as **Trotton**, **Chithurst**, and **Iping** on the western reaches of the Rother recorded major flooding in 1962 and drew up a detailed history of floods going back to 1871. There was some concern in 1903 when **Easebourne** warned local parishes that the War Office was proposing to 'turn the Sewage from Longmoor Camp into the source of the Rother in an only partially

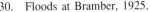

30. Floods at Bramber, 1925.

31. Slindon Pond, *c*.1910. The house on the left was one of the boyhood homes of writer and poet Hilaire Belloc.

purified condition'. **Rudgwick**, in the days of the Vestry, recorded the washing away of Wanford Bridge's parapet by floods in 1852.

Ponds can be hazards, too. **Slindon**'s parish council inherited the village pond when it took over from the Vestry in 1894, and in 1897 a special parish meeting was called to approve a doubling of the threepenny rate to pay for cleaning out the pond and strengthening its base. Further cleaning was needed in 1905, when the rural district council told them that was the only way of eliminating the pond's disgusting smell. Presumably matters improved, as there were five refusals to requests to fish the pond between 1919 and 1924. But the saga continued: in 1927 the county council cleaned out the pond,

32.   Bob Dudden working the ferry at Bury, 1931.

as it was a useful sink to draw storm-water off the highway. By 1928 the water was thick with flannel weed: the parish consulted the curator at Kew, who told them to put some copper sulphate into a bag and drag it across the pond behind a boat or on a long pole, which they did. Did it work? Well, by 1947 they had put up a sign prohibiting boating and bathing but allowing paddling, which implies that people actually wanted to do so.

Ponds are often central to villages and many have been the subject of attention to celebrate national events. **Milland** chose the present Queen's silver jubilee as an ideal occasion to turn a sludgy bog into a delightful woodland duckpond beside the road, where the water tumbles away into an old sheep-washing pond known as The Plug. But ponds also attract dumpers, and in the parish of **Bosham** there is a continuing rumble about rubbish being dumped into the historical Bullrush Pond, reputedly built as a reservoir to supply a Roman encampment under Vespasian, commander of the Second Legion.

Bury, on the river Arun, is quite possibly unique among West Sussex's inland parish councils in that it had a parish wharf, where at the turn of the century it agreed to build a boathouse. A ferry plied to and fro across the river.

Greens, Commons and Rights of Way

Every parish has had its problems with open spaces and rights of way over the years. **Northchapel** used to have regular arguments about pigs, cattle and horses running wild over the green and through the churchyard. (Whatever happened to village pounds? **Amberley** parish council was discussing ownership of the pound in 1938; **Cowfold**'s Vestry meeting was expanding the pig pound back in 1854.) **Aldingbourne**, in 1897, persuaded the Hon. Mrs. Denman to transfer the fence she had recently erected, enclosing roadside waste, to the ownership of the parish council, which then ordered a brand, marked APC, so that it could brand each fencing post and also a stopping post to prevent cattle entering the enclosure.

Rustington had its Battle of the Gates. In 1908 the owner of the manor house, Mr. T. Bushby, claimed ownership of the adjoining Pigeon House Lane by putting locked five-bar gates at either end of the lane. After much debate, one of the parish councillors (Mr. T. Summers) declared that the lane was a public right of way and that he would personally take an axe to the gates. The locals watched in amusement as Bushby and Summers alternately put up and demolished the gates until, in desperation, Summers formed up a procession behind the Rustington Silver

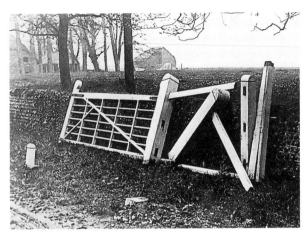

33.   Rustington's 'Battle of the Gates', 1908.

Band and marched to the gates, chopping them down again with great ceremony. Bushby withdrew from the fight.

West Wittering parish council's long-running dispute about Snow Hill Green ran on for 25 years. The parish suffered, indirectly, from commonland inclosures in the late 18th century which led to the creation of straight roads—the well-known Birdham Straight, incidentally, is said to have been marked out originally by a Mr. Wells, who ploughed the longest furrow in Sussex. The drawback to straight roads in a modern age is that motorists cannot resist putting their foot on the accelerator. To compound the problem, land under the freehold of the Church was turned into a car-park by a tenant farmer in the 1920s—he was able to make quite a few bob because Schneider Trophy seaplane races took place on the Solent, and his field was the competitors' turning point: an ideal vantage point for the crowds that came to watch. In due course, with the car-park well established and luring holidaymakers who took advantage of Wittering's long stretches of beach, the freeholders took over the area from the tenant farmer and built a new road to it, before selling the land to a private company in 1952.

The Witterings were also involved back in 1877 when the **Birdham** Vestry meeting got together with the Witterings and with **Earnley** to exclude cattle from grazing along the roadside.

West Sussex has many other seaside parishes and some are jealous guardians of their shores. **Pagham** actually owns two sections of foreshore, where it has put in concrete hardstandings with public seating and a walkway so that wheelchair-users can reach the raised beach. It was quite a battle: they eventually acquired the land by means of a compulsory purchase order after a saga which lasted for 14 years. With persistence, a parish council can do it!

Burial Grounds

Some parish councils have very little to do with churchyards in the parish, apart from perhaps a regular financial donation to their upkeep. Others are much more involved in their management, which is a link with the old Vestry days. **Billingshurst** parish council manages the graveyard and faces major problems: the churchyard was closed 20 years ago and it is not possible for people to be buried within the parish today, though the parish council is working very hard to find a suitable site. **Cocking** was told by Midhurst RDC in 1951 that its graveyard had been contaminated by smallpox—it supplied a note of various epidemics in the 18th and 19th centuries, and surely many a parish had exactly the same problem. **Lavant** parish council, in 1903, expressed great concern over a proposal by the parochial church council of St Mary's in East Lavant to extend its graveyard: the parish council decided this would create a health risk for the adjoining school and two cottages whose occupants used a well which might become contaminated by decaying corpses. This was a parish council which in its early years discussed whether a urinal was necessary for use by allotment holders as well as a water-pump, and to which a complaint was made in 1919 about soapsuds and other dirty water being thrown into the road by various householders.

In 1900 **Poynings** parish council agreed that 'it was time that something was done' about the churchyard, where human remains were being exhumed when new graves were dug. They used exactly the same phrase three months later, and over the next four years their meetings were dominated by the complicated business of closing the churchyard, negotiating with the Local Government Board to establish a burial board, finding and acquiring a cemetery site (for £35), surveying the grave plots and constructing a perimeter wall, and setting a scale of fees for burials.

Light, Gas and Electricity

The old Lighting & Watching Acts seem to have caused considerable controversy in some parishes, where the arguments for and against their adoption were argued over many years. Many rural parishes today still stiffen at the thought of 'suburban' street-lighting, but in the past perhaps the stiffening of local residents was more at the thought of having to *pay* for such lighting, especially in days when a man was employed to light each lamp by hand and then extinguish each one during the night.

The High Weald village of **Ardingly** attracted more than a hundred people to a parish meeting on 17 October 1896 to decide whether or not to adopt the Lighting Act. At a show of hands, only five voted in favour, and it was not until another parish meeting some 60 years later

34. Billingshurst's favoured site for a new burial ground. The remains of Hammond's Mill might be converted into a chapel.

that the Act was finally adopted: they decided to pay for eight electric lamps out of a Coronation Fund donated by Wakehurst Place's Sir Henry Price (of 'Fifty Shilling Tailors' fame).

In **Pulborough**, they had voted a sum of £55 for street-lighting at the end of 1914 but the time was wrong. The subject was raised again in 1918 when they resolved: 'The Home Office having withdrawn the lighting restrictions, the question of lighting the street lamps for the ensuing three months having been discussed it is agreed that the Lamps be not lighted.' Yes, that's right—*not* lighted. The ratepayers, having found that they could live without street-lighting during the war, felt they could continue to do so during the peace. It was not until the winter of 1923 that Pulborough's lights were turned on, when they were converted from 30 oil-burning lamps to '150 candle power petrol burning lamps'. They would go electric in 1932 with the help of the Steyning Electric Light Company.

Thakeham was still arguing about lighting areas in the early 1960s when, at an annual parish meeting, an attempt was made 'from the floor' to persuade the parish council to support a demand for a certain lighting area. Feelings apparently ran high for a while but order was restored eventually and, in the words of one with a long record of service on the parish council, 'Thakeham, after the initial excitement, relapsed into its almost medieval past!'.

Billingshurst has been dealing with the problem of lighting for a hundred years and is alarmed to find today that it must spend many thousand pounds to convert some of its street lights to county standards along main roads. **Henfield** installed some gas lights in the 1870s and the parish council extended these in 1912; they were replaced by electric lighting in 1934. **Storrington** had electric lights three years later, and **Hurstpierpoint** by 1939.

Lavant parish council was discussing the possibility of having gas supplied to the village back in 1909: gas mains were laid at last throughout the village in 1992. Yet **Crawley** was lighting its streets by gas as long ago as *1859*, when its population was less than 500 people and

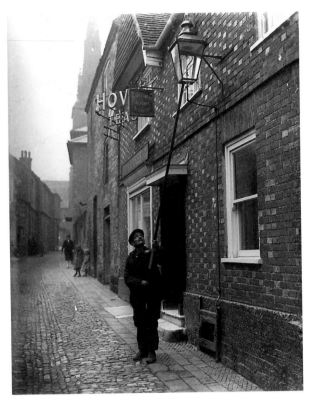

35. *(Left)* Richard Carver, Petworth's lamplighter, in Lombard Street, 1931.

36. *(Above right)* Servicing the lamps at Pulborough, 1932.

schoolmaster James Gibbs of Ifield was the paid Assistant Overseer whose jobs included collection of lighting rates. The duties of Crawley's lighting inspectors were handed over to the parish council in 1921. Crawley had a fire brigade in the 1860s; it also had a 'father' to whom it erected a memorial in the Centre Square in 1872. This was Mark Lemon, editor of *Punch*.

Post and Telephones

Northchapel's early parish council guaranteed to the postmaster that it would meet the deficit of operating costs of the telegraph (about £7 per annum) in order to keep the facilities open for the village. In 1899 the subject of postal facilities was discussed at **Barnham**'s annual parish meeting. That was the same year in which **Washington** parish council authorised its chairman to write to the Postmaster General asking on what terms he would grant the parish a full post-office (94 years later Washington's post-office and shop are in trouble). In 1908 the parish of **Bepton** was a little alarmed at newspaper reports of a half-holiday for postmen, and the parish of **Poynings** was informed loftily by the National Telephone Company that there was insufficient support for a telephone service to its village. In the summer of 1923, several parishes received a letter from the postmaster at Haywards Heath about an application from sub-postmasters and postmen for a half holiday every Wednesday. The parish councils were not at all happy with that idea—**Twineham** said it would miss its daily papers on Wednesdays (delivered by the postmen) and suggested that an auxiliary postman should be engaged to relieve the regular postie.

Â Â Â Â Â Â Â **Aldingbourne** could measure its population growth by the fact that in 1899 its parish council was moved to demand a second daily postal delivery. **Bersted** had *three* daily postal deliveries in the 1920s, and a telephone was installed for the parish council at the post-office in 1925. **Stoughton** bettered them all: its own parish clerk was the postman, delivering mail from a donkey cart.

37.   Byworth's post-office, with public telephone, 1931.

38.   Tom Mills, postman, at Westbourne, 1920s, in the days when the mail came up from Emsworth.
He was then clerk to Stoughton Parish Council.

Housing

Vestry minutes sometimes refer to parish cottages and these were handed over to the parish councils in many instances. The parish cottage at **Compton**, for example, was sold by the parish in 1906, while **Slinfold** still had a Parish Cottages committee in the 1930s. **Bersted** gave potatoes grown at its parish cottages to the poor who did not have gardens; in 1829 it conveyed the lease of one of the cottages to the Rev. Edward Eadle as he had bought new almshouses for the parish.

Housing for 'the workers', as opposed to the poverty-struck, became a popular theme in the villages very early in the life of the parish councils. At a parish meeting in **Ardingly** in 1896, a councillor presented a petition signed by some of the parish's inhabitants asking 'for the erection of six Workmen's dwellings' and the meeting resolved to request the district council to 'apply to the county council to obtain power for the erection of Cottage Dwellings under the Housing of the Working Classes Act 1890'. Between the 1930s and 1974, some 128 council homes were built in the village of Ardingly; and in 1993 the parish council asked for support from the district council and the district housing association to build eight or ten dwellings for rent in the grounds of Hapstead House (which was the property of the county council).

Parish Property

Many parishes already had recreation grounds and similar open spaces dedicated for the enjoyment of the parish's inhabitants in the 19th century—usually with a strong Victorian motive of improving their health and, somehow, morals. That theme of 'improvement' extended to the creation of parish reading-rooms or simply 'parish rooms'. This idea developed naturally into village halls as meeting places for all sorts of events and groups, and also to the establishment of a few public libraries by parish councils. **Lavant**, eager to look after the intellectual as well as corporal health of its parishioners, was discussing its 'parish library and reading room' right from the start; **Slinfold** had a parish library committee even before it had a parish council; and many parishes already had reading-rooms, stocked with newspapers and journals as well as books. Other parishes in the very early days of their councils sought to 'improve' people through adult education: **Amberley** parish council was discussing the provision of lecturers under the Technical Instructions Act 1897; **Sompting**'s parish council archives include accounts of the Sompting Night School for the late 1890s; and **Eastergate** had a Cheese School between the wars. All parish councils, of course, elected governors to their local schools—which continues the old Vestry tradition.

39. Eastergate Cheese School, 1927. Instructing students in the use of the cheese press.

COWFOLD WAR MEMORIAL.

AT the meeting held in the Village Hall on Monday, May 26th, a Committee was formed with instructions to ascertain as nearly as possible the approximate cost of Alms Houses and a Lych Gate.

Your Committee having gone into the matter, believe the following figures to be a fair guide:—

ALMS HOUSES.	£	LYCH GATE.	£
Alms Houses comprising 3 tenements, viz., a central house of 2 stories, 3 bedrooms, kitchen, sitting room, and larder, with attached offices		Lych Gate, comprising:—	
		Building Gate, Walls, erection of Memorial Tablet	600
A cottage on either side including bedroom and kitchen on the ground floor with detached offices ...	1500	Purchase of Land :—	
		Rebuilding adjoining Property	800
Purchase of land	100		
Endowment, including rents, rates, taxes, repairs, and insurance ...	1000		
	£2600		£1400

*Willing to Subscribe*_____   *Willing to Subscribe*_____

Signature _____   *Signature* _____

Those desirous of supporting either of these Schemes are invited to state the amount they are willing to contribute under either of the two columns.

Please return this appeal by Friday, August 1st, at latest to

C. B. GODMAN.

Mr. T. H. Gates,
Homestead,
Cowfold.

PRICE & CO., PRINTERS, HORSHAM.

40. Cowfold's memorial appeal after the First World War.   41. Eastergate Parish Hall.

42. One of the murals in Eastergate Parish Hall. This one commemorates Dick Newland, the 'father of cricket', who lived by the pond in Slindon. Other murals, by artists such as Byam Shaw and Barbara Chamier, show a series of historical Sussex scenes and characters.

Many a parish formed a quite separate committee for the purpose of establishing war memorials. Wars and jubilees were often the incentive to open meeting places of various kinds in the parishes, whether recreation grounds, sports pavilions or halls. Indoor meeting places sometimes developed from estate and village rifle-ranges which had been built when the Boer and other wars had highlighted a certain lack of shooting skills. **Eastergate** built an elaborate combination: its parish hall, opened in 1908, had a main hall for meetings and concerts, with two 27-yard rifle ranges built into the side aisles and overlooked by a spectators' gallery. This was no ordinary hall: its sights were set much higher than WI meetings and bazaars. The emphasis was very much on the arts and this fine hall was decorated with frescos and paintings by Byam Shaw and other artists, showing historical events in Sussex—at Selsey, Cowdray Park, Arundel Castle, Houghton, Walberton, Slindon and Eartham for example. This splendid hall was later donated to the parish by its private owners.

Another impressive hall is that of **Henfield**. In 1921 the parish council purchased the Assembly Rooms in the High Street (using a loan of £1,800—Henfield, like many parishes, relied very heavily on loans) which provided the village with a parish hall, parish office and council chamber. The Assembly Rooms were sold in the 1970s and, with another loan, a superb village hall complex was built in 1974, including a large hall with a stage, a small hall and committee room, catering facilities, a parish office—and even a special room for the parish museum, open to the public. The museum had evolved in 1948 in the Assembly Rooms, based initially on a collection of mostly domestic objects donated by Miss Lucy Bishop and her aunt, Alice Standen. The collection continued to grow, so that in 1993 a larger room and proper storage were built for it.

These two large halls are in great contrast to those of many villages, but the more humble are just as vital to their communities and just as well used. Mrs. Mercy Hunt, who spent her childhood in **Rudgwick** (and had many happy memories of the village), moved with her new husband to **Lyminster** in 1923 and became thoroughly involved in local affairs and organisations. All the meetings were held in the Parish Room—parish council meetings, church councils, Men's Fellowship, Sunday School, sewing meetings, Guides and Brownies, the WI, billiards, socials, the Men's Club, whist drives and so on. The parish room was the centre of village life.

43.   Billingshurst Village Hall, opened in 1991.

44.   Mrs. Irene Marshall at work. She has been clerk to Billingshurst Parish Council since 1987.

East Preston could have had a Peace Hall in 1919 but it didn't happen. The parish council minutes, as is so often the case, revealed very little of the true story of the peace hall saga but it happened that there was a far less reticent scribe to hand: the pseudonymous 'Scribble', whose little local newspaper gave all the gossip. There had been debate throughout the war as to whether a memorial should be a new church organ, other church restoration work, or a village hall. The Vestry proposed church restoration as soon as the war was over, hence the hasty convening of a parish meeting to propose a more secular village hall. Both sides voiced willingness to co-operate but only insofar as making an appeal for *both* schemes, in conjunction. As a result, donations went mostly to the church and the idea of a much needed hall quietly died. It took several decades before pressing need made the village hall a reality: they converted an old tithe barn into a three-hall complex for the village, and the East Preston and Kingston Village Hall was at last opened in 1981.

Harting is another parish which took a while to build a hall. For many years it 'made do' with various small and ill-equipped premises but these less than perfect venues were regarded with affection by many in the village, so much so that they managed to scupper two post-war attempts to secure a decent meeting-place. It was not until the early 1980s that the parish council purchased a site from the district council and, 'in the face of wavering support and unfounded fears among parishioners about the difficulties of raising the money', the project was finally brought to fruition—largely due to the determination of the parish council's chairman, Air Commodore North-Lewis, and its clerk, Ken Hughes.

East Preston War Memorial.

Our readers will remember in our last issue we called attention to the fact that we had heard no more about the scheme for the Village Memorial as distinct from that adopted by the Church. The whole idea seems to have "fizzled out."

Although we were on the Committee and were quite prepared to have done our share towards the erection of such an institution, we have as yet heard nothing more. East Preston has the distinction of having done something, of course, through its Church, in honour of the memory of those fallen in the Great War, but this is not enough. We ought to have a permanent building, in a suitable part of the parish, which can be an everlasting reminder to us that those who have fought, and bled, and died, did a great deal for those who follow. The Y.M.C.A. Hut which has been erected, and which is now nearing completion in the Recreation Ground at East Preston, will serve no doubt as a temporary measure, but this is not vested in the parish, although we understand its use will not be stringently restricted for use by the villagers and parishioners. We hope that the scheme, upon which there was such a lot of controversy, will not be allowed to remain idle and drop out, but that the temporary building can be used to give concerts, entertainments, and bazaars, the proceeds of which should go towards the Memorial Fund to enable the parish to erect a suitable and permanent institution worthy of the same.

45. The East Preston saga, recorded by 'Scribble' in 1919.

Middleton-on-Sea also limped its way to a hall. Most of the original village is now under the sea (the parish now has a 'Rock Island Line' to hold back flooding) and most of the present village has been built since the First World War: Captain H. R. S. Caldicott returned from the war with a large gratuity and bought a considerable part of the land of Manor Farm, including along the sea-front, and residential development began there in 1921.

Middleton has had a parish council since 1928. An appeal for £8,000 to build a King George VI memorial hall in 1953 petered out despite initial enthusiasm—it seemed that the village couldn't care less and they only raised about £1,300. They tried again in 1977 with rather more success: they reclaimed the original funds from the Charity Commissioners and eventually their new hall was opened by Lavinia, Duchess of Norfolk, on 1 September 1982.

The village hall at **Fernhurst** became involved in a tragedy. The hall was founded in 1909 'for the use of the inhabitants of the Parish of Fernhurst and the neighbourhood thereof without

Price—One Shilling   № 72

Souvenir Programme

The

MILLAND VALLEY MEMORIAL HALL

SATURDAY, AUGUST 7th, 1948

OFFICIAL OPENING

FOLLOWED BY

A FLORAL FETE

in the Field opposite "The Rising Sun"

HALL TO BE OPENED AT 2.15 P.M.

BY

The Rt. Hon. **HUGH GAITSKELL**, M.P.

MINISTER OF FUEL AND POWER

ADMISSION IS BY THIS PROGRAMME
KEEP IT!   YOURS MAY BE THE LUCKY NUMBER

46. A celebrity opens Milland's Memorial Hall, 1948. Hugh Gaitskell had property in the Valley where, although he was Minister of Fuel and Power at the time, he and the rest of the village relied on well-water and paraffin lamps.

distinction of political, religious or other opinions, including use for meetings, lectures and classes and for other forms of recreation and leisure-time occupation with the object of improving the conditions of life for the said inhabitants.' This clause was typical for many village halls which were managed under charitable status—one of the main planks is that they must be open to all, regardless of 'opinions' and persuasions. But in 1967 it found a rôle which could hardly have been envisaged by its founders.

It was on Bonfire Night that a Caravelle airliner crashed into a field on Blackdown Hill, killing all 37 passengers and the crew. Fernhurst became the centre of rescue operations and locals worked closely with the emergency services that were quickly on the scene. The Youth Club became a canteen; a village shop offered provisions; the post-office supplied hot drinks; and individual villagers supplied sandwiches and a rota of staff in the canteen, as well as offering accommodation for any relatives who might have to come and identify the deceased. This was 'emergency planning' put to the practical test in the most appalling circumstances. The village hall became a mortuary until the bodies could be removed to the mortuary at King Edward VII hospital, Midhurst.

The memorial hall at **Colgate** is another with a tragic history. The original village hall was destroyed by Luftwaffe bombing in 1940 in a horrific and senseless raid that also damaged several homes, the post-office and the church and killed five people. After the war the parish waged a long battle in its claim for war damage and eventually was given £1,900 in settlement, which became the basis of a fund-raising campaign to rebuild the hall. It was finally opened in 1953, due largely to the willingness of local craftsmen to contribute their labour and skills without charge.

Tangmere is a parish which has changed greatly twice: once because the RAF moved in, and then again after the Ministry of Defence sold its airfield and a large number of ex-servicemen's homes. A lot of land was released for development; new industries became established and many new houses were built. During the 1980s a public meeting gave the parish council a clear mandate to investigate the provision of a village centre. They came up with an ambitious scheme for a main hall large enough to seat 150 people, another smaller hall, a kitchen and storeroom, and changing facilities for sports players. It was paid for with the help of substantial grants (the district council was particularly generous) and included a separately financed and purpose-built medical wing with surgeries for doctors and dentists, various clinics and a dispensing service.

The little village of **Wivelsfield** managed to raise £16,000 in four years of coffee mornings and annual fairs towards its new village hall, opened in April 1981 because the village had outgrown its old reading-room (built in 1912). Sale of the reading-room realised £20,000; the rest of the costs were met with substantial grants.

47. Destruction of Colgate Village Hall by German bombing, September 1940.

Colgate Village Hall, former Church School, after a direct hit, Sept.10th 1940 (from a photograph)

Burgess Hill has a drinking fountain, erected in 1872 in memory of Captain William Pigott by his widow 'for the benefit of poor wayfarers': she set it on a piece of ground she had acquired 'formerly part of the waste of the Manor of Keymer'. Mrs. Pigott then bought shares in the Burgess Hill and St John's Common Water Company so that the fountain would be well supplied with 'wholesome fresh water'. In due course trusteeship of the fountain was vested in the hands of Burgess Hill UDC and the fountain continued in existence, joined by a horse trough. But the fountain became a traffic hazard at the junction in more modern times and was removed somewhere around 1970. Much later it was rediscovered, in several pieces, under a forest of stinging nettles in the district council's Parks depot and nobody seemed to know much about it— or care. The town council thought it would be nice to resurrect the fountain to celebrate the Queen's silver jubilee in 1978. Easier said than done. The site they chose was in front of St John's church but the county council refused permission—the land was designated as highways land. The town council counterclaimed by pointing out that the original site of the fountain had been commandeered by county when it was making a roundabout and had assumed the land was county's. Touché. They did a swap of little bits of land; the pieces of fountain were reconstructed on the new site and surrounded by paving and seats, and the old horse trough rejoined its old partner and was planted up with flowers.

Slaugham's 'antiquity' was My Ladies' Bowl, a piscina or water-bowl with a long history. The spring near Furnace Pond, which still produces 'an inexhaustible supply of chalybeate water', had long been prized when some of the women of the Covert family, of old Slaugham Place, ordered the creation of a bowl, neatly chiselled out of a big slab of sandstone, to ensure a perpetually clean and readily available source of water from the spring. That was during the 17th century; two centuries later, local volunteers ensured that the bowl was kept clear of mud and fallen leaves. (After all, the springwater had once been so well-known for its health-giving properties that in the early 1800s a man would come over from Horsham with a dog-drawn cart to collect a barrelful of the water as an eyewash.) In the early 1980s, the county council decided to concrete it over in the interests of safety. Local historian and now honorary citizen of Slaugham, Roger Ray, managed to fight off such an insult and the bowl remains.

Aldingbourne had an even more dilapidated and far more ancient piece of property, though it did not realise it. This was a castle, no less—or, rather less as it turned out. It was a mound. The inimitable Les Coker, whose fund of knowledge as a West Sussex parish clerk is profound, had always assumed that the mound might be 'one of those underground shelters much loved by the Royal Observer Corps' until one day he received a letter asking if the parish council

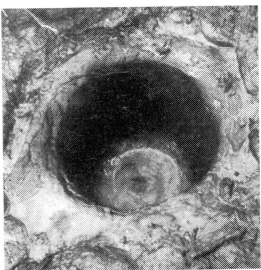

48. *(Left)* Pigott's drinking fountain 'for the benefit of poor wayfarers', Burgess Hill.

49. *(Above right)* My Ladies' Bowl, Slaugham, carved from sandstone. This photograph dates from 1927. Today the bowl is hidden by a fallen tree.

would mind if the writer explored the mound with his metal detector. Coker could see no reason for involving the parish council and suggested that the writer should contact the landowner, whoever that might be. In due course he noticed evidence of little excavations here and there about the field close to the site and idly wondered how much treasure the metal detector had unearthed. Treasure? He perked up. He looked at the Ordnance Survey map. It referred to the mound as a 'Castle'. Another map said it was a 'Bishop's Mound'. Then out of the blue a parish councillor from the past delivered a package to Coker dating back to long before his own time as clerk. Inside was a beautifully drawn plan of the mound site and a copy of a solicitor's letter referring to a conveyance of the site to the parish council years earlier. No one on the present council knew anything at all about it but it was true: in 1969 the site had been purchased by the parish council for the 'rest and recreation' of its inhabitants, for a sum of £100. Looking into its history, he discovered that it had indeed once been a castle, of motte and bailey type, and the home of a bishop for a while.

Fancy a parish council owning a castle unknowingly! But then, how many parishes know what lies hidden in their own archives?

Other parishes are lucky enough to be given land in various forms. **Rogate** seems to receive bequests of land quite frequently—recreation grounds, for example, and pieces of woodland, and Olivers Piece which was bequeathed by an elderly inhabitant because she liked to sit there and look over the Combe. **Harting** is another landowner of the same kind: in 1937, for example, by a Deed of Gift the late Sir Philip Reckitt of Littlegreen entrusted the parish council with some 14 acres of wood and parkland for perpetual use by local residents as a recreational area, beauty spot or timber reserve. Most of the land is woodland, known as the Warren, and serves as a wildlife haven. A substantial area of the woodland was cleared in the 1940s and replanted by the parish council with beech as the Wace plantation (it was named after the council's chairman of the time, Sir Blyth Wace). Then in 1988 the parish council bought two ponds on land

50. Les Coker, clerk to Aldingbourne Parish Council since 1979 and to several others over the years. He also worked in the County Council's offices and is an expert on commonland, *inter alia*.

51. The site of Tote 'Castle', Aldingbourne— more than a mere mound.

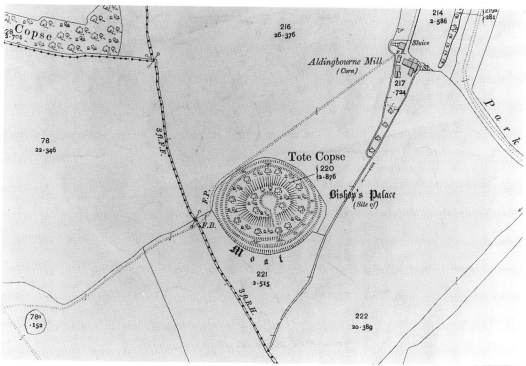

52. South Gardens, Harting, a parish council's ponds and parkland.

immediately adjoining the original parkland known as South Gardens; the purchase was financed by an anonymous donor but the council paid for improvements to the site and has a Parkland Management Board which is responsible for looking after the Warren and South Gardens. Most of the work is carried out by a small but enthusiastic band of volunteers.

Clocks are sometimes the concern of parish councils—not so much clock-watching as clock-care. **Steyning** had a three-faced village clock, installed just after the formation of the parish council, which had been gently falling to pieces for years and finally jammed its mechanism in 1985. The parish council diligently sought a specialist company to make new faces but shuddered at the quote of more than £2,000. The day (or rather the clock) was saved by local signwriter and artist Clifford Carter, who did the job in his spare time at cost price, with no charge for his labours. The final bill was about a tenth of the original quote.

At **Yapton**, the parish council was more interested in bells, and contributed £250 towards two new treble bells at St Mary's church in 1985.

Parish property can be of the symbolic kind. The wife of the late chairman of **Cocking**'s parish council is the proud possessor of a very frail old banner of the Cocking Friendly Society; in dark red silk with a broad blue edge and fringe, its central medallion on one side shows a sickroom scene, and the reverse has a large blue bell dated 1876. (The old friendly societies were in effect the forerunners of insurance companies and, in a way, of the national health service.)

Several West Sussex parishes have chairman's badges. **Fernhurst** was presented with one by Mrs. Merrett in memory of her late husband, Harry, who had died in office in 1976. This badge was designed by a former parish clerk, Richard Pape, and its four quarters include the church, a deer (representing local wildlife), a signpost (indicating the parish's network of footpaths) and farm implements. **Steyning** created a chairman's badge to celebrate the royal wedding in 1980, an occasion which **Lancing** celebrated by improving facilities for the disabled.

Many parishes have symbols decorating their headed notepaper and some of them are reproduced in this book to inspire others. **Birdham** (which also owns a ship's bell, presented by their namesake HMS *Birdham* in 1967—it now hangs in the primary school) has quite an elaborate logo, again divided into four quarters representing various aspects of the parish. It was devised by way of a competition at the primary school in 1989 and the winning design was given to a heraldic designer for refinement. **Clayton**'s two windmills are beautifully reproduced on the parish council's notepaper; **Thakeham** has a splendid green oak (the parish council is justly proud of its successful life-saving of a grand old oak near Rydon school and the imposition of tree preservation orders on an evergreen oak at Abingworth and an avenue along Merrywood Lane); **Eastergate** naturally boasts a lion's head (again as the result of a local competition) to match its war memorial. **Worth**'s symbol is less obvious: it was designed by local teacher and historian Jeremy Hodgkinson, formerly a member of the parish council, and cleverly represents what were originally the three parts of the parish—Copthorne (a gorsebush), Crawley Down (a shaded tree for its woods and an anvil for its former iron workings) and Turners Hill (a lychgate for its church and four compass points suggesting its crossroads). **Turners Hill** became a separate parish with its own parish council in 1986 but Worth retains the original logo 'for old times' sake'.

53. Steyning's three-faced clock.

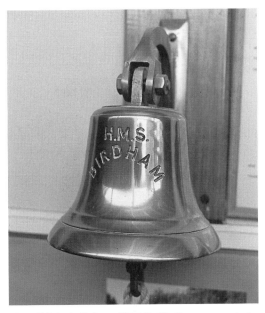

54. Ship's bell from H.M.S. *Birdham*, presented to Birdham.

Burgess Hill is one of the few to have Armorial Bearings, granted to it in 1953 in its former guise as an urban district council and transferred to the new town council in 1975. Its symbolism includes a wall, a vase and a potter's wheel to represent the clay products (bricks and pottery) which were its original industries; a grassy hillock suggests local scenery; and the Sussex connection is in the bird above the hillock—six gold martlets were the arms of the old kingdom of the South Saxons. **Henfield** also has its own coat of arms, granted in 1992 and inspired originally by the parish council's chairman, Peter Hudson, and the village's Roman Catholic priest, Father Mark Elvins, an expert on heraldry. The design was produced by a local resident, Mrs. Brenda Hobbs, who works with the College of Arms, and it includes a golden oriel sitting on a thorn bush (commemorating the family of botanist William Borrer, whose descendant is reputed to have seen a flock of oriels in a thorn bush), the crossed keys of the parish church of St Peter's, and the Corpus Christi pelican in her piety to represent the Catholic church.

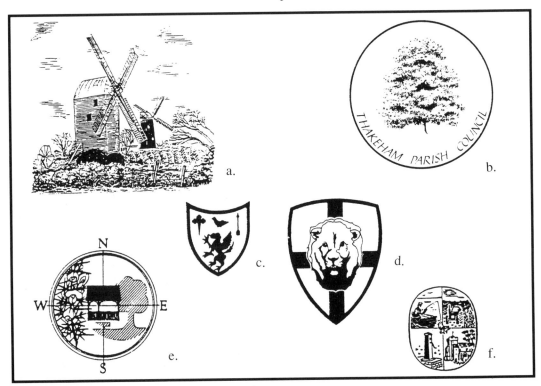

55. Several parish councils have devised their own logos. This selection of letterheads includes: (a) Clayton; (b) Thakeham; (c) Bersted; (d) Eastergate; (e) Worth; (f) Birdham

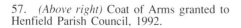

56. *(Above left)* The armorial bearings of Burgess Hill's urban district council, now transferred to Burgess Hill Town Council.

57. *(Above right)* Coat of Arms granted to Henfield Parish Council, 1992.

58. *(Right)* Great seal presented to Lurgashall Parish Council in 1895 by the 'Right Honourable Lord Tennyson'.

Lurgashall is perhaps the grandest and most unusual of all: the parish council has a great seal so massive that it takes two to carry it to every parish council meeting for sealing documents. The seal was presented to the council at its birth: it is marked 1895, and the presenter was Lord Tennyson. There is a slight mystery here: Alfred, Lord Tennyson, lived at Blackdown and always took an interest in the village, but he died in 1893. Perhaps he ordered its making before he died?

Arundel, as a town council (which, incidentally, must hold a record for the shortest ever meeting—precisely six minutes in 1983), has all sorts of mayoral paraphernalia. By 1987 the ceremonial hats worn by male councillors had become so tatty that they refused to wear them, and it was formally agreed that they no longer needed to do so. In 1985, at a reception to welcome the 27-year-old Earl of Arundel, the town council almost beat their own 1983 record: the preceding meeting was over in seven minutes, which left them plenty of time to be presented with a new town crier's bell by a couple who ran a local estate agency. In 1983, to celebrate the 500th anniversary of the dukedom of Norfolk, the current duke was made an 'Honorary Mullett' ...

Chapter 5

On the Move

It used to be said that the women of Sussex had exceptionally long legs, as a result of the constant struggle to drag their feet out of the winter mud. And they had only the parish to blame! Until the 20th century, it was always thought that roads were strictly the concern of those in whose area they were and that the parish, a unit more stable than even a kingdom, was ideally placed to look after them. Sussex's roads were considered to be the worst in the country.

Parishes had been highway authorities, responsible for and bearing the cost of the repair and maintenance of their own roads, since 1555, though the counties were responsible for bridges (which came under the care of county surveyors responsible for public buildings). Most Vestry meetings appointed their own highways surveyor, whose only essential qualification was honesty and who was obliged to serve, if so elected by the parish, for one year. Until 1835, the post carried no salary.

In 1862 Justices of the Peace (in effect, the county) were given power to form unions of highway parishes as Highway Boards for the sake of greater efficiency. The actual cost of highways works devolved on the local parishioners who, not surprisingly, began to object when through traffic increased their financial burden. Subsequent Acts spread that burden over whole districts and introduced grants to help as well. In 1888, the newly created county councils were given full control over main roads; other highways in rural areas became the responsibility of the district councils in 1894.

The parish surveyor's task was an arduous one. Since 1555 the system had been based on statute labour: certain people in the parish were bound to supply a cart with a team of oxen, horses or donkeys and labourers with necessary tools when the surveyor needed them. This system persisted until statute labour was finally abolished in England in 1835, when the cost of highway repair and maintenance became a charge on parish rates. But in many parishes local farmers and tradesmen continued to make available their carts and animals to carry road materials as needed, and later to hire them—a practice which continued well into the 20th century.

Local roadmen in each parish were responsible for particular lengths of road. It is in human nature to take a pride when given a sole responsibility and those roadmen did just that. They were also well aware that everybody in the parish knew them by sight and name as well as by reputation, which was an added incentive to do the job well. They were familiar local figures, and so were the stone-breakers whom many older villagers today can remember sitting at the crossroads with a large heap of road stones, gradually reducing them to smaller pieces with a hammer.

SYMONDS BRIDGE.

NOTICE IS HEREBY GIVEN,

THAT A MEETING WILL BE HELD

On Friday, the 21st day of December, 1855,

AT THE THREE CROWNS INN, AT WISBOROUGH GREEN,

AT TEN O'CLOCK, OF THE

OWNERS & OCCUPIERS

OF LAND, WITHIN THE

TYTHING OF DUNHURST,

In the Hundred of Winterswrith, in the County of Sussex, and of the
Owners of Thirteen Copyholds of the Manor of Amberley, for the
purpose of making a Rate upon all such Occupiers, for the repair of
SYMONDS BRIDGE, in the said Parish of WISBOROUGH GREEN. The
Timber for the repair of one half of which Bridge is by custom supplied
by the Bishop of Chichester, and the Workmanship by the Tenants of
Thirteen Copyholds in the Manor of Amberley, and the other moiety
as well of Timber as of Labour is by custom supplied by the Inhabitants
of the Tything of Dunhurst.

THE ATTENDANCE of all OWNERS and OCCUPIERS of Land
within the said Tything of Dunhurst and of the Owners of the said
Thirteen Copyholds is particularly requested.

The Chair will be taken by John Napper Esq., of Ifold; who has
kindly consented to explain the state of the case.

HENRY HARWOOD,

Wisborough Green, 14th December, 1855.   HARSFOLD.

A. J. BRYANT, PRINTER, PETWORTH.

59. Poster summoning ratepayers to a meeting about repairs to Symonds Bridge, Dunhurst, in the parish of Wisborough Green, 1855. Now known as Simmonds Bridge, over the the River Kird, a tributary of the Arun.

60. Country lane, Wiston, 1933.

Each lengthsman was responsible for about 15 miles of road, which he tended with barrow, shovel, broom and faghook, and the roadman's brushfire after he had been tidying the verges was a common sight by the lanes. He was quite prepared to instruct local landowners to trim back their roadside hedges, too. He knew every grip and ditch and local troublespot.

There was a considerable reduction in the number of roadmen after the Second World War: they were being replaced by mobile gangs which became increasingly mechanised. Maurice Milne, West Sussex's county surveyor from 1960 to 1968 (now retired to Bosham), remembers setting up teams in vans, ready to tackle any job, under the direct control of a district foreman. The last of West Sussex's lengthsmen retired before 1970.

Traffic

Rural roads were still swirling with summer dust or sticky with impossible winter mud well into the present century. For several centuries it had

61. Jigg Hill, the Petworth roadman, 1932.

been the practice to 'lay' summer dust simply by watering the roads, but the invention of new forms of transport proved to be too severe a test for such techniques.

Until 1896, the maximum speed for other than horsedrawn vehicles on a highway was walking pace—4 m.p.h. Then the speed limit was increased to 12 m.p.h. for a 'light' vehicle of less than three tons. By the same legislation in 1896, the motor car was first legalised as a road vehicle, and the first London/Brighton run took place that November. Life in the lanes was about to change for good, and the dust began to fly. A national Automobile Club was formed in 1897 and soon motorists would be agitating for road improvements.

In fact they had been preceded long since by cyclists, who formed a Road Improvement Association in 1886 when the punctures and potholes had become unbearable. Among them was a cyclist living in **Wivelsfield**, who decided to do something practical about laying the dust that made cycling less than a pleasure. He was Rees Jeffreys (author of *The King's Highway* and Secretary of the Road Board, which preceded the Ministry of Transport) and his idea was that tar was a better dust-layer than water. He therefore ran a competition for inventors of tar-laying machines. West Sussex was clearly at the heart of progress in road-making: Rees Jeffreys at one stage was offered the chairmanship of Lord Cowdray's company, Highways Construction Ltd.

By 1910 tar-spraying was widely used on highways for laying the dust, which was just as well: in 1903 the speed limit had been increased to 20 m.p.h., which really sent the dust

62.   Road-making at Partridge Green, *c*.1900.

63.   Cuckfield High Street, *c*.1910. Note the rough state of the road surface.

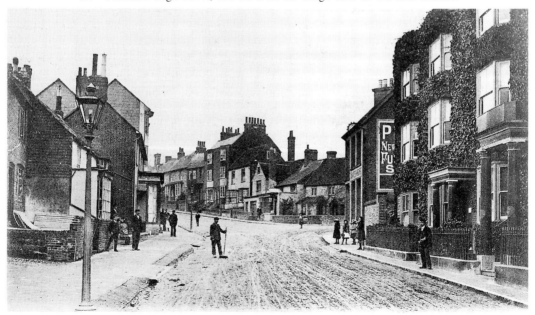

64. Nurse Wake of South Harting striding the Downs above the village on her rounds, 1920s. The signpost marks a familiar junction today and a point of controversy over a proposed bypass in the early 1970s.

flying—and sent people flying too. Speed traps were set up in towns, and the Automobile Association took steps to warn its members of these sneaky tricks.

The idea of motoring quickly caught on among those who could afford private cars and they wanted tarmac and asphalt on the roads. With the better surfaces for motor vehicles the rate of road traffic accidents (many of them involving pedestrians) became very high compared with the number of vehicles. An Act in 1934 introduced driving tests for the first time and a 30 m.p.h. limit in built-up areas, and the first Belisha beacons were seen. The counties took a look at their areas to decide on where the new speed limits should apply; and Dennis Bostwick, now with West Sussex's traffic department, still has the original map of the county's first speed limits.

The first white lines down the middle of the road appeared here and there in 1925 but came into their own in 1939-40, when they were painted on all trunk roads as 'aids to movement' during the wartime blackouts. A signing system had evolved in the early days of motoring but had been nothing to do with government, whether central or local. It was the AA and RAC who put up signs to help their members—how to get to wherever, how to know when you had got there, and what hazards to watch out for along the way. Fingerposts were around by the 1920s.

The Road Traffic Act of 1930 empowered the highway authorities to cause or permit traffic signs to be placed on or near roads, and it became an offence to do so unless the signs were of a size, colour and type prescribed by the Ministry of Transport. In 1964 signing was the subject of a complete revision by a special Ministry working party, and the design of signs became uniform all over the country.

****

That, then, is the background. What was actually happening at parish level? It is well worth reading, first of all, through old Vestry minutes: every parish clerk should do so, and will find a wealth of information about the history of local roads, often down to every grip and ditch and drainage problem.

Roads, and the traffic that used them, remained a constant theme after the parish councils had been created. So many parishes mention roads as being of major concern throughout their

65.   Station Road, Cowfold, early in the 20th century. It is now the busy A272.

66.   An Austin 'Chummy' crossing Bay Bridge, near Dial Post, 1927. Today the same river crossing is made by the A24 dual carriageway.

67.   Balchin's Garage at Fittleworth, 1930.

history that it is impossible to cite all of them here, but speed limits, dangerous roads, motorcycles and bypasses are recurring problems.

As early as 1902, **Aldingbourne** parish council was drawing the county council's attention to the 'dangerous state of the road at Westergate Street between the Railway Crossing and the *New Inn* ... in these days of motor cars and to avoid accidents needs speedy amendment'. In 1910 they asked for a 10 m.p.h. speed limit in the same road but this was turned down. Then in 1913 they asked the district council to 'tar the road through Westergate' and also notified district of 'a nuisance arising from the washing of carts in the narrow portion of Westergate Street near the Green'. Nine months later they were still asking for tar, 'having regard to the dusty condition of Westergate Street during the summer months, also its filthy condition in the winter, consequent upon the large and increasing motor traffic'. They asked again for the street to be tarred in 1915 and, at last, in 1917 they noted 'with satisfaction the action of Westhampnett

68. An AA Scout, somewhere near Fittleworth, 1930.

District Council in repairing the road through Westergate Street and trust that the tarring of the road will be proceeded with immediately as the great amount of car and heavy lorry traffic is seriously injuring the new surface of the road'. Two years later (oh yes, the saga continues), they resolved to send a letter to the district council 'to tar Westergate Street as soon as possible'. In 1971 the parish council was once again fighting for the improvement of Westergate Street for the safety of pedestrians and of 'fast vehicular traffic'.

Chithurst was another persistent parish on the subject of the small parish's few lanes. In 1899 they were querying the amount of stone used on their highways and were told that it was an annual average of just over 175 cubic yards during the last five years. In March 1900 this parish meeting put in one of many formal complaints to the district council about the state of the road through Borden village. Stone was the subject again in 1905 when they wondered 'when the Stone now on the roadside, put there some of it in 1903 and broken in 1904, is to be put down', and they resolved 'to point out that the Patching done this Winter was pure waste of Material'. In 1936 they were still distressed about the state of the lane through the village and at last something was done about it, after 30 years.

Poynings started trying to reduce the speed of traffic through its village in 1905, when they passed a resolution declaring that 20 m.p.h. was excessive and dangerous to public safety. In 1911 the parish council complained that 'locomotives on the highway were a great source of danger' but the county council reassured them that such vehicles were prohibited from

69. Old traffic signs awaiting restoration at the Amberley Chalk Pits Museum, which also exhibits old road-making techniques and materials.

pulling more than three wagons. Poynings had asked for danger signals in 1909 but was rejected; and when they asked the AA to provide 'Notices of Caution' in 1922 the county council got shirty and said that it was the only body authorised to erect danger signs. So Poynings asked for four of them. Seven months later nothing had happened. Before and after the Second World War they pleaded for 30 m.p.h. speed restrictions and were rejected; in 1946, in despair, they told the clerk to put up his own 10 m.p.h. speed limit sign. The outcome of this little rebellion is not recorded.

Northchapel fared rather better: the AA provided it with 'Caution Boards' through the village as early as 1903; ten years later they were discussing speed limits of 10 m.p.h. but today speeding traffic remains a problem. **Slindon** was another urgently requesting a speed limit in the early days—in 1907 it wanted one of only 6 m.p.h., which was perhaps optimistic. **Twineham** supported **Keymer** parish council 'in every way' in 1905 in its attempts to 'secure a limitation of speed of Motor Cars through the Village Streets of the County. This Council regrets that a wider view of the question was not taken.' They also called upon the county council to urge the government to contribute towards the upkeep of the main road (the A23).

In 1907 Twineham parish council received a letter from Cuckfield RDC 'with regard to communications from the County Council with respect to giving a tar surface to the main road'—provided that half the cost was contributed locally. In 1912 they called the attention of the county council to 'the large increases in the amount expended on the Main Roads and as most of the wear is caused by through Traffic which does not contribute towards the upkeep, the Parish Council suggest that the County Council should press for the nationalisation of the chief through roads, especially the main London to Brighton Road. The Parish Council have the opportunity of seeing the enormous heavy motor traffic pass through from London to Brighton.' By 1922 they were worried about the danger at Hickstead crossroads; six years later they were told that a subcommittee would deal with the matter but they had to write again about the extreme danger at the crossroads in 1931. Lo and behold, in 1952 the clerk was again being instructed to complain about the dangerous conditions at Hickstead crossroads! In 1925 the problem was the 'inconvenience' caused by large charabancs using unsuitable lanes, and in 1933 it was the slipperiness of the roads, especially dangerous for agricultural horses.

Slaugham, in 1906, was the scene of what was until then the worst motoring accident in Britain: a top-decker motor bus whose passengers were on an annual fire-brigade outing from Kent passed through Handcross High Street at 12 m.p.h. heading for Brighton and, seven minutes later, ten of its 36 occupants were dead or dying. The unfortunate driver's footbrake had failed at the start of the hill on the Brighton side of Handcross.

Bersted's was less dramatic—a cycle accident at the end of the 19th century led them to ask for improvements to the Chichester road between North and South Bersted. In the Vestry days there had been a great deal about Bersted roads.

Many a West Sussex village has tried over the years to have itself bypassed by heavy and speeding traffic, and sometimes they have succeeded. Back in 1928, it was proposed that a new 'motor road' or 'motorway' from London to Brighton should be built along the former turnpike road that ran through the parish of **Albourne**. The parish council strongly opposed the proposal as it would 'cause grave disadvantages to the parish, cutting through several fields making them useless, running through the whole length of the parish'. Among the members of the parish council at the time was one Sidney Hole, a farmer, businessman and prolific inventor who, during the early 1930s, took it upon himself to look after the interests of 78-year-old Julia Proctor. She was almost blind and her business and home, Tipnoak Cottage, lay in the path of that proposed new road.

70.   Bus accident at Mid Lavant, 1931.

71. Sidney Hole, long-serving Albourne parish councillor and inventor. When he died at the age of 89, in 1956, he held 70 patents, including one for a well-known coding machine.

72. Sidney Hole's famous Manulectric trolley. He also invented a spillproof, thiefproof and dirtproof milk churn.

Well, they did pull down the cottage—but the county surveyor, in compensation, rebuilt another cottage for the old lady in the same style as the original, using the same materials as far as possible, and paying particular attention to the interior so that she would be able to find her way around in apparently familiar surroundings. That is quite an example of the human face of 'them'!

There is a final twist to this little tale. Although Sidney Hole did not realise it at the time, in the 19th century Tipnoak Cottage (then known as Woodbine Cottage) had been the boyhood home of another Albourne inventor, James Starley (died 1881), who became known as the father of the cycle industry. The rebuilt cottage, now again called Woodbine Cottage, is now the home of Inez Dann, who was clerk to Albourne parish council from 1988 to 1992. As for the 'new' road of the 1930s, it became the A23 and earned the nickname Blood Alley—it was so dangerous that, due largely to the determined efforts of the parish council and its chairman, Commander John Lewis, a new Albourne bypass was opened in 1991.

The demolition of old cottages was also necessary for the realignment of the A24 in the parish of **Washington**. The debate over the proposed route began in 1961, and led to a degree of ill-feeling between the parish council and the county council. It seems that there had been a public enquiry ten years earlier at which the parish had raised no objections to a western route, passed by the Ministry of Transport in 1953, but no record of this was found in the minutes of either the parish or the district council. However, the western route it was and, although it meant demolition of the parish's tennis courts as well as the cottages and the compulsory purchase of private and National Trust land, in hindsight the general opinion seems to be that the right route was chosen.

Another successful bypass campaign was that launched by **Westhampnett** in the 1960s, a parish of three hamlets—Westerton, Maudlin and Westhampnett, the latter two suffering considerably from heavy traffic. Part of the bypass was opened at last on 26 July 1993 and the parish looks forward to celebrating not only its centenary in 1994 'but also the chance to return to a village environment'.

The bypass proposals for **Harting** became probably the most divisive issue ever to come before its parish council. The arguments began in the early 1970s—not about the need for a bypass, which was universally desired, but about its route. The county proposal, claimed

73. Tipnoak Cottage, Albourne, in its original form; once the home of James Starley, inventor of the two-seater 'Social Tricycle' and the differential gear. Tipnoak is the name of one of the old hundreds.

74. View at South Harting. The route of the proposed bypass would have cut across this scene and scarred the downland slopes.

the parish council, 'would have slashed through a local farm and The Warren and South Gardens, ruining one of the ponds and probably damaging the springs that feed Harting Brook—a tributary of the Rother. Having looped round the village it would have delivered traffic to the existing roads at the foot of the Downs. To ease the passage of traffic up the steep Chichester road, the county engineer proposed to create a deep cutting through the shoulder of Harting Hill—the resultant white scar, he glibly assured parishioners, would soon be concealed by regrowth of grass and other vegetation.'

Harting was not happy and a substantial group of villagers argued for a more expensive route along existing rights of way from high ground west of South Harting along the top of the Downs, flanking the South Downs Way, to minimise loss of farmland, avoid scarring the landscape, and to eliminate the problem of traffic on the steep north face of Harting Hill. The 'discussions' sometimes became heated to the point of acrimony. And all to no purpose: there was no money for any sort of bypass in the end. The village continues to be concerned about the damaging effect of traffic through its midst, particularly heavy goods vehicles, and the county council has recently introduced experimental traffic-calming measures to reduce speeds. Some other villages in the county are also grateful recipients of such measures in the last two or three years.

It is not only villagers who worry about speeding traffic. In **Walberton** the likely victims are ducks: several had been killed crossing the road as they waddled from their nesting area on the village green to have a swim on the village pond. In 1987 there were about 70 resident ducks and local people (especially children) were increasingly upset at finding the birds' dead bodies in the road. The chairman of the parish council, Don Milburn, therefore designed a 'Ducks crossing' sign to warn motorists of the hazard.

Nice idea. But the county council promptly removed them, saying that they were unauthorised signs. Mr. Milburn said they were on private land and they were back in place within hours. County said it would make special signs to a design approved by the Department of Transport, but it would have to seek permission from the Department to have three or four signs along the road. Ah well, these things must be done properly, mustn't they? Actually Mr. Milburn's own sign was rather charming.

This is a good example of what seems to parishes like unnecessary niggles and interference in parish affairs, but, after all, the highway is the responsibility of the county council now and it is bound by Acts of Parliament which decree that all road signs must conform to the national norm.

Tucked away in the archives for **Stoughton** parish council is a revealing letter about signs. It was sent, presumably to all parishes, from West Sussex County Council's divisional surveyor's office on 24 January 1952, as follows:

Village Place Name Signs

It is proposed to erect village place names throughout the County and for this purpose I enclose herewith a small map upon which I have marked the approximate position of the signs affecting your village. At each of the points marked in red on the map will be placed a peg. These pegs will have silver tops and the grass verge around the pegs will be cleared so you should have no difficulty in locating them. All pegs will be in position by the 26th inst. If any of your committee have any observations, please let me know before 2 Feb, when the erections will be starting. It should be pointed out that all signs will be erected in positions clearly visible to the road user and that the object is to include the developed areas of the community and in no way to define the parish boundary.

Bus services are another typical cause for concern in parishes, especially in recent times. But even in 1949 **Twineham** parish council was being informed by Southdown Motor Services that the village's bus service was running at a loss and its future would have to be considered. The clerk was instructed to inform the company that the parish council 'thought that one of the objects of the Nationalisation of the Transport Services was that the losses incurred in thinly populated districts could be offset by profits from more populous areas'. Well, **Harting** had an answer to that many years later, as described in the final chapter.

Many parish councils put up and maintain bus shelters: **Upper Beeding**, for example, chose a bus shelter as a way of celebrating the Festival of Britain in the 1950s. **Steyning** parish council had the constructive idea of involving its grammar school sixth-formers in the Best Kept Village competition in 1983 by asking them to decorate the bus shelter with a mural. It depicted St Cuthman pushing his elderly mother in a wheelbarrow—after the legend that a wheel fell off when he reached Steyning and so he settled there.

From such earthy matters, some parishes turn their eyes skywards and worry about aircraft. **Tangmere** became quite attached to its airfield and the presence of the RAF, but **Twineham** parish council, in 1934, was none too happy with a proposal for an aerodrome at Bolney on land adjoining its parish and made a protest to the Ministry of Air pointing out that the aerodrome would be 'detrimental to the peaceful amenities of the district' and also a danger to the public. Two years later there was a lecture in the village hall to explain 'arrangements in connection with the general scheme of Air Raid procedures', and of course the Second World War broke out within three years. In 1941 this little parish (population 295 today) was told that, in the event of bad air raids in Brighton, Twineham would be expected to accommodate 62 evacuees.

Thakeham is another parish with aircraft problems and the parish council received countless complaints at one time about the noise and general nuisance of low-flying fighter planes.

Slinfold Station, L. B. & S. C. Ry. Sussex.

75. Slinfold railway station, *c*.1910. It was one of many that would suffer under Beeching's axe in the 1960s.

On the ground, the railways brought so much to so many rural areas in the 19th century, and also brought commuters in their many thousands to West Sussex in the 20th. The devastating axe wielded by Beeching in the 1960s has had consequences far greater and more disastrous for the villages than perhaps have been appreciated. But some have benefited, especially where stretches of old railway line have been converted into bridleways and footpaths. A final quote from the minutes of **Lavant** parish council's meeting on 13 May 1986:

> Resident on the Old Railway Track - It has been reported that a 'gentleman' together with a 'lady' are residing in a tree house built in an evergreen oak on the Railway Track near Oldwick Meadows. His presence is causing some concern as the man in question sometimes gets 'worse for drink' and this tends to frighten people. There is also concern over the 'health aspect'.

The next chapter looks at some of the characters in the history of the parish councils—and I am not claiming that the above gentleman was a retired councillor or clerk.

Chapter 6

Characters

Any parish council or parish meeting is the sum of the individuals who participate: it is sometimes forgotten that 'the' parish council, or 'they', is not an anonymous body but a group of real live human beings with names and faces and with greatly differing characters and philosophies. It is time to look at some of the actual people who have served parish councils over the years—and in some cases over very many years.

In **Eastergate**, William Collins (born in 1844, died 1935) was chairman of the parish meeting from 1894 to 1928, Overseer of the Poor from 1894 to 1902 and chairman of the parish council from its inception in 1906 and for the next 18 years. He was born at Decoy Farm, Tangmere, one of ten children in a farming family, and became a yeoman farmer, a grocer, a butcher, a postmaster and a general businessman: he was the proprietor of the Elm Tree stores in Eastergate and owned a number of properties in **Aldingbourne**—where he became a member of the first parish meeting in 1894. He was still chairman of Aldingbourne parish council in about 1910 and was re-elected in 1913, though thereafter his name seems to disappear from Aldingbourne's minutes. But years later his grand-daughter, Mrs. Bertha Stewart Watson, started attending parish council meetings as a member of the public and became a member in 1966, chairman from 1977 to 1983, and a co-opted member in 1986—she remains

76. William Collins of Eastergate (*see also* Fig.25), with his wife Harriet and family.

very active on environmental matters for the parish today and has served on an impressive number of its committees. Her historical knowledge of the parish is unparalleled.

Twineham parish council's first chairman was Mr. R. W. McKergow ('elected to the chair at ten minutes past six' on 4 December 1894); in 1934 the minutes recorded the parish council's congratulations to Colonel McKergow on his appointment as chairman for the 41st year and thanked him for his services during the past 40 years; in November 1947 tributes were paid to the council's late chairman, the Colonel, and it was agreed to co-opt his widow as a member of the council and to appoint her as chairman.

Another public-spirited man was Conrad Coombes of **West Wittering**, who served for many years as a churchwarden, parish councillor and chairman of the parish council and also as a district councillor, in an era which saw the advent of the motor car among many other major changes in village life. Mr. A. G. Cate followed a family tradition in West Wittering: he served for two periods of office on the parish council, his cousin George Cate had served on it from 1905 to 1930, and his grandfather was probably the last parish constable appointed by the Vestry.

Henfield is another parish council which stretches family connections over the years: two doctors Lewis (father and son) were elected in 1894 and the practice was bought in 1932 by Dr. H. F. Squire who became a parish councillor five years later—his son, Dr. John Squire, is still a parish councillor today. And the local fruit-farming family, the Whittomes, can boast some 70 years on the parish council—Eric Whittome for 40 years and his son

77. Henry Thomas West, JP, chairman of Henfield Parish Council from 1894 to 1904. His house is now a home for retired clergy.

78. Eric Whittome, on Henfield Parish Council for 40 years.

79. Mrs. Heather Grant, who was still an active member of Cuckfield Rural parish council when she died at the age of 93. She had lived in Ardingly until moving to Cuckfield in 1946, and was elected to the rural district council four years later.

80. Roger Ray, 'Honorary Citizen' of Slaugham.

Donald for 29. In the combined parish of **Stedham-with-Iping**, the current chairman Eddie Lintott was delighted to report at Stedham's 100th annual parish meeting in 1993 that two of his own relatives, Alfred and Frank Lintott, had been elected to serve on the parish council at the first meeting on 4 December 1894 and that the original minute book was still in use.

At neighbouring **Trotton-with-Chithurst**, Alastair Robertson has been on the parish council since 1938—a remarkable spell. But perhaps the prize goes to the late Mrs. Grant of **Cuckfield Rural** parish council: she served on it for many years and was still very actively involved at the time of her death in November 1993, although she was by then 93 years old; she had also served on Cuckfield RDC and was a well-loved and vigorous supporter of village life in all its aspects.

Some parishes honour their long-servers in various ways. Roger Ray, for example, was made an 'honorary citizen' by **Slaugham** parish council at its 99th annual parish meeting: he is not only the local historian but also its longest serving parish council member (though he is only 76 years old) as either a councillor or its clerk. He also served on Cuckfield RDC, for 11 years, and Mid-Sussex DC for 15 years, and his wife was once the parish council's clerk as well. He had joined Slaugham as parish clerk at the tender age of 29, after the Second

81. John Wood, Lindfield's Swan Master, feeding Charles and Diana on the village pond in 1985 with the help of the 2nd Lindfield Brownies, who raised funds for new pond posts.

World War, and was its chairman for 18 years until 1989, after which he continued as a parish councillor.

Harting decided to approve, 'quite unofficially!', the creation of two Freemen of Harting: Major General L. A. Hawes and Mrs. Phyllis Hosking, both of whom had served the local community with distinction for many years, including as parish councillors. But even Harting was not in a position to appoint anybody as a Swanmaster. This post at **Lindfield** traced back to the 19th century (there was even a Mr. Masters in the post from 1911 to 1913—a period when there were complaints about the high cost of the swans' corn), but the appointments lapsed when the parish council was abolished in 1930. Fifty-five years later the Friends of Lindfield Pond revived the idea: the two resident swans, Charles and Diana, welcomed Mr. John Wood, a breeder of cagebirds and caretaker of King Edward Hall, to his new responsibilities.

Pulborough has drawn up an intriguing list of the names of people who took some part in the affairs of Pulborough parish council or its annual meetings from 1895 to 1946, with details in many instances of not only length of service (several for half a century or more) but also their occupations and addresses—a veritable social history of the parish.

Some of West Sussex's parishes have had a few famous names on their councils or among their residents. **Keymer**'s famous personalities included Magnus Volk, son of a German clockmaker and an eminent electrical engineer who built the first electric railway in Brighton in 1883, and another railway on stilts (known affectionately as Daddy Longlegs) from Banjo Groin to Rottingdean in 1894. Volk stood for election to the parish council in 1907 but failed; three years later he succeeded and remained on the council until he resigned just before Christmas 1914.

Bosham was the home of Gerald Marcuse, the renowned radio amateur and a pioneer of Empire Broadcasting; when he died in 1961 the Radio Society of Great Britain commemorated his achievements by presenting the parish council with a splendid teak seat in his honour.

Another famous Sussex name is that of the artist and craftsman Eric Gill, who began his career with an interest in lettering but later became famous for his sculpture—for example

82. Magnus Volk (1851-1937), pioneer of lectrical engineering and a Keymer parish ouncillor.

83. A Magnus Volk creation: 'Daddy Longlegs', the sea-going car of the Brighton and Rottingdean Electric Tramroad, in 1898.

in Westminster Cathedral—and his designs for war memorials. In 1909 he wrote to Keymer parish council on behalf of Keymer Land Club asking them to provide four smallholdings for the club's members—he was living in Ditchling High Street at the time and in 1993 a new gallery housing a collection of his memorabilia was opened in Ditchling Museum.

Keymer parish council had a lot of trouble with its clerk in the early days. Mr. E. F. Hope, Assistant Overseer as well as parish clerk, resigned formally in March 1909 after the auditor had discovered substantial 'discrepancies' in his accounting—including £280 11s. 5d. in the rates accounts and £27 0s. 3d. in the allotment accounts. Their fingers having been burned, the parish council took a long time to appoint a new assistant overseer and clerk, though there were 13 applications for the post.

Most clerks are rather more reliable, and many serve for a very long time indeed. They can be difficult to trace, at least from minute books, as they are often too modest to name themselves there. However, many of the first clerks were named in their parish's entry in the 1895 edition of Kelly's *Directory of Sussex* (which is a treasury of detailed information about each parish). In the early days they were often the Assistant Overseers, on their modest little salaries which might or might not be enhanced by another even more modest little salary as clerk to the parish council. And in the early days they were always men. How things have changed!

In April 1896 one Arthur Martin was appointed as Assistant Overseer and Clerk to the parish council of **Amberley**, at a salary of £20 per annum. He was by no means a local man: in fact he was already in the same two posts at Seaton, Kettering, where he had also been 'Collector for the Surveyor of Highways'. One wonders why the council could not find a Sussex inhabitant for the job but he duly moved down to Amberley lock, stock and barrel—

84. In memory of Gerald
Marcuse, at Bosham.

85. Harting war memorial,
by Sussex sculptor Eric Gill.

his effects including a printer, for which the council was only too happy to find accommodation, though it was written that 'we could let it stand on the Waggons, or store it in the classroom, or somewhere else until the house is ready'. It seems that the new clerk would in due course reside in the schoolhouse. From the grand formality of a warrant appointing an Assistant Overseer for **Cowfold** in 1895, clearly such a post was not lightly undertaken.

In old **Treyford** churchyard, site of the demolished 'Cathedral of the Downs', there is a cast-iron gravehead inscribed: 'JOHN CHALLEN 30 years Parish Clerk fell asleep Mar 17 1875 aged 74. Jesu Mercy. A faithful and trusty official'. He was, of course, the church's parish clerk rather than the parish council's and one of his jobs was to keep the congregation awake—perhaps a job which also sometimes falls to a clerk to the parish council.

The clerk to **Eastergate** parish council, W. T. Cole, served in the post for 42 years, from 1926 to 1968, and was also postmaster at Slindon—was he the same postmaster who served as clerk to **Slindon** parish council for 39 years? The latter, a keen cricketer (and later umpire), was appointed Extra Assistant Overseer in 1898 to 'legalise his appointment', when he asked for and was granted a rise in salary from £3 to £4 a year. That was the last rise he ever had, though he was presented with a silver inkstand when he finally retired in 1936. In contrast, J. W. Turner resigned as Slindon's clerk after only one week in 1945,

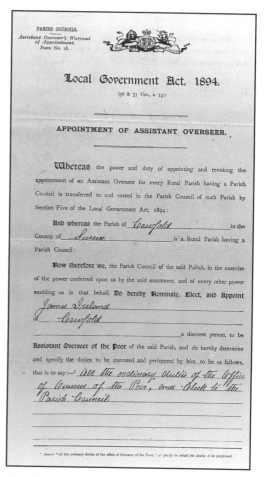

86. Part of a document (dated May 1895) appointing an Assistant Overseer at Cowfold, with a yearly salary of £50—he was also appointed clerk to the parish council.

apparently because he had failed to persuade his council to organise VE celebrations on a grand scale (he was captain of Slindon's Home Guard). Other Slindon clerks included a headmaster, an agent for the local estate, a solicitor, a solicitor's clerk, a retired civil servant and an industrial economist. The first woman clerk at Slindon was appointed in 1983 (a year before clerk Bernard Keeling published his history of the parish council), which is much later than in several other parishes. Today a high proportion of West Sussex clerks are women.

Slindon's postmaster was not the only clerk with postal connections. Tom Mills was **Stoughton**'s parish clerk for many years and he also used to deliver the mail in a donkey cart during the 1920s.

Birdham's clerk 'Dickie' Dickinson served for more than 40 years before retiring in 1989. W. J. G. Dixon served as clerk to **West Chiltington** parish council for 39 years; and John Hill did the same for **Westhampnett** for 41 years, from 1949 to 1990, during which time

87. John Hill, clerk to Westhampnett Parish Council for 41 years, at his retirement presentation in 1990.

88. Clarence Linton, MBE, clerk to Tillington Parish Council since 1931. He was formerly clerk to the parish councils of Kirdford (1935-78), Plaistow (1935-81) and Rogate (1940-75).

he was employed by the Goodwood Estate and was much involved in running the racecourse and the motor circuit in its heyday, as well as the Duke of Richmond's country estate (Goodwood's land takes up much of the parish).

The chairman of the old **Cuckfield** parish council wrote a letter to its clerk, Mr. Plummer, on 30 March 1948 as follows:

> I cannot tell you how sorry I was to receive your notice to relinquish the position of Clerk to the Cuckfield Parish Council which you have so faithfully carried out for such a long period (52½ years) which I think must be a record. My fellow councillors also express their deep and sincere regret and join me in wishing you good health and every happiness in the future. We shall all miss you very much, also the valuable help and advice you have always been able to give and we thank you from the bottom of our hearts.'

Cuckfield had only six clerks in its first hundred years, but Mr. Plummer's long run must have rather upset the averages.

Harting has had only four clerks since 1949—schoolteacher Bill Greetham for 20 years, followed by the versatile Don Francombe (retired July 1981) who was a classics master, versifier, writer and producer of plays, writer of reviews, author of a booklet on the history of Harting, a chorister, press correspondent, editor of the Parish News, and founder of Harting Music Club. He was followed for ten years by Ken Hughes, who retired in 1991.

Rogate has had only three clerks during this century: the present one, Mrs. Margaret Bentall, has already served for 19 or 20 years, and her predecessor for about the same period.

Ardingly was served by only three clerks in 87 years: the first, Henry Munnion, was the Assistant Overseer and continued in office until 1904, when his son Ernest H. Munnion took over as clerk and stayed for the next 54 years: he was awarded the MBE, though some clerks today might suggest the honour should have been a VC! His successor was Clive H. Izard, clerk for 24 years at his retirement in 1981 and who remains on the parish council today.

Balcombe produced a family succession when Will Gardner took over as clerk to the parish council from his brother John, who was emigrating to New Zealand, in the early 1960s. Will had lived in Balcombe all his life and was very popular there. He never wrote down anything—he never took notes at a meeting but used a tape-recorder instead. If anybody spoke of anything other than what was on the agenda, it was erased from the tape. His slogan seemed to be that 'a nod is as good as a wink' and he would always do the job, whatever it was, albeit in his own good time. He never got ruffled and managed to see a funny side to most situations—a saving grace in any parish clerk.

There was a family theme among the clerks to **Thakeham** parish council, too. The first was John Rapley, head teacher of the old Board School, who served as clerk for more than half a century, from 1894 until the early 1950s, and every page of the minute book for the period is in his handwriting. He was presented with an illuminated address on his retirement. He was remembered well by Mr. Skinner, a council member for 40 years to 1976, whose daughter was clerk for ten years. Mr. Skinner's grandfather (born in 1837) had been a parish constable in the Vestry days, and a paternal uncle had been an early parish council member.

Littlehampton appointed an ex-footballer as its town clerk in 1981: Dennis Goodwin had played for Everton. **Chichester** claimed to have the oldest town clerk in the country (let alone the county) when Eric Banks retired on his 80th birthday in 1981. **Tillington** can beat that. In 1993 Clarence Linton wanted to resign as clerk to the parish council but his resignation was refused. After all, he was only 82 years old. He had been in the job since he was 20 and his experience was far too valuable to lose. An oak tree on the Upperton road already marks his 60th year as clerk.. When he retired as clerk to Plaistow parish council in 1981 (after 46 years) they gave him a party and a silver-plated salver.

Coldwaltham is unusual in that its clerk is possibly the only one in the county who quite literally links the parochial and the civil councils, which is strange in view of the evolution of parish councils from the Vestry meeting. The Rev. Clifford Stride is a non-stipendiary priest in charge of Hardham church. He took on the post as clerk to the parish council two or three years ago and feels that it provides him with 'opportunities to keep all aspects of the community life together'. The idea seems to work very well for Coldwaltham and one wonders why it is so rare. An example of the harmony between parish council and church is the use of the church's Sandham Hall as a post-office. The parish, a combination of Watersfield, Hardham and Coldwaltham, had become shopless until the Post Office in Brighton agreed to the creation of a 'cubby hole' in Sandham Hall in 1990, open three mornings a week. The chairman of the parish council is the postmaster and on one of the three mornings the vicar runs a coffee shop, which provides a social occasion for the village and also sells produce for church funds.

The job of clerk to the parish council has changed, especially in recent years when it has become more complicated and even more demanding. The volume of paperwork has certainly increased hugely, and attitudes to the job have changed as well. Whereas in the past perhaps most clerks looked upon parish council work as something of a sideline which kept them involved in the community, for very little salary, there is a growing trend towards

89.   The Reverend Clifford Stride *(left)*, clerk to Coldwaltham Parish Council, with his chairman Peter Beresford who is also the village post-master.

90.   Coldwaltham's 'cubby hole' post-office in Sandham Hall.

greater professionalism and an interest in taking quite challenging training courses and comparing notes more widely with other clerks. It is doubtful that the clerks of today will stay in the job as long as their predecessors: the population as a whole is far more fluid, for a start, and there is also the problem of expectations. Parish councils are notoriously bad at producing sensible 'job profiles', and that can lead to dissatisfaction on both sides.

Judy King, clerk to **Clayton** parish council and brand new to the work (so her eyes are very clear), analysed a 'diary' of the comings and goings of clerks in her parish and concluded that there were two main factors in a period of rapid turnover: that in the past the job was taken on almost as an honour for which people were almost pleased to be reimbursed for postage stamps, and that the amount of time involved and the constant demands at all hours of the day and night are rarely anticipated. Her analysis over the last 40 years included a senior valuation officer, whom they paid £104 p.a. for 25 hours a month in 1967 and who resigned after four months because the duties involved were 'more numerous' than originally envisaged (this clerk also worked in London all day). The next clerk had been a secretary (increasingly the trend in clerks since the war); she stayed for six years and was followed by a housewife with 9 'O' levels. Within a few months of her appointment, the chairman of the parish council was writing to the National Association of Local Councils drawing attention to 'what appears to be a vast anomaly introduced by a proposed new Parish Council'. This referred to an article in the *Mid Sussex Times* about **Burgess Hill** parish council, which had decided to employ a full-time clerk at what Clayton regarded as a 'fantastically high and unrealistic salary' of £3,000 p.a. This parish council would replace Burgess Hill's urban council in April 1974 as a result of the Local Government Act 1972.

Clayton's chairman continued as follows:

The work of this new parish council will not be any greater than that carried out by most councils, which in turn are served by part-time clerks who have devotedly given their time and energies to their parish duties for slender reward. Often their salaries are only a token payment in exchange for the generous care with which they perform their functions, and the majority consider their posts as a vocation to the community and not as a means for monetary gain. This splendid attitude of clerks, which is much admired, would be completely undermined by a reactionary approach such as that envisaged by Burgess Hill which goes entirely against parish council protocol and would, if implemented, reflect abjectedly upon every loyal clerk throughout the country. It is obvious that this is the town thinking of an Urban District Council which has had no dealings in the past with Parish Council affairs, and has not acquainted itself with the functions, background and running of such councils. Its approach to this subject is still at UDC level, with no regard for its effect on other parish councils... I understand that your Association has published recommended rates of pay for parish clerks which give a maximum salary of less than one third that proposed by Burgess Hill ...'

A year later Clayton's clerk resigned; the post was advertised and 49 applied for details but several said the pay was too low for the number of hours of work expected (one calculated the rate as 45p per hour, compared with a rate of 60p at least for any old clerk-typist). Well, Clayton did appoint a new clerk in May 1975, and another one in July—and another in October! The latter stayed for some 18 months and resigned because it was more time-consuming than expected. The next one lasted 10 months and was followed by a shorthand-typist, who at last settled into the job and stayed for 14 years. When she finally stood down in 1993, there were 24 applicants for details of the post. In May that year Judy King, previously an office administrator and secretary, became the new clerk to Clayton parish council. We who are or have been clerks to parish councils wish her all the best—there is a great deal of satisfaction to be had from the job, even if the financial rewards are minimal!

Chapter 7

Initiatives

The aims of this centenary history are twofold: first, to describe the past as the context for the present, and second, to inspire parish councils with even greater enthusiasm as they step into the next hundred years—with a new millennium on the near horizon. This chapter gives some examples of initiatives that have been a little bit special, something more than the many everyday achievements of every council in West Sussex.

Several parish councils have worked hard for many years to meet the growing need for affordable homes for their villagers. Recently they have begun to succeed, usually in co-operation with their district council and with various housing associations. Among them, by way of example, is **Milland**, which was often close to giving up in despair during more than a decade of pleading for homes for its older inhabitants and also for the young whose families had lived in the valley for years and who could no longer compete with an increasingly affluent and mobile population of newcomers. That Milland did succeed was due largely to the unstinting efforts of its then district councillor, D'Arcy Burdett, and its unsung heroine, Miss Emily Lawrence, who had lived in the area all her life. It was with great pride that Milland welcomed the Earl of March in 1989 to open Strettons Copse, a pleasant little group of 11 small homes for rent at the heart of the village built by Chichester Diocesan Housing Association. The neighbouring parish of **Trotton-with-Chithurst**, its population of 250

91.   Strettons Copse, Milland, affordable homes for young and old.

being a quarter of Milland's, is just about to build six affordable housing units of its own after some three years of negotiations. The experience of these and several other parishes seems to be that co-operation between two or three levels of council, sometimes joined by a generous local landowner willing to supply a site at a reasonable price and almost always involving a housing association, is the key to meeting affordable local housing. And co-operation it must be: it takes a great deal of work and dedication on all sides and a lot of persistence from the parish council itself.

Amberley parish council, in 1981, was instrumental in saving the village's surgery. Public support encouraged the parish council to form a charitable trust to buy the building, and the fund-raising began in earnest. Within a few months they had raised more than the asking price by a combination of private donations and the income from 14 special events in the village.

The **Harting** Minibus is a classic example of village enterprise. In the early 1970s the general decline in public transport prompted the rector, Roy Cotton, to suggest a village minibus. The parish council formed a steering committee with the rector and other volunteers. They made full use of the traditional annual Harting Festivities in 1972 and managed to raise almost two-thirds of the sum needed for the scheme they had devised. An anonymous loan ensured that 'Daffodil' was soon on the road, driven by a group of volunteers who had all passed special tests. In those days, fares were not allowed and so operating costs had to be met by more fund-raising ventures and donations—and the rector came up with the idea of a village Tote, the weekly proceeds to be divided between the bus funds and the prize money. The parish council set up a management committee and today the Harting Minibus (several buses newer than the original one) still runs a regular scheduled service to Petersfield and Chichester. It was one of the first such schemes in the country and its committee chairman, Roger Bricknell, visited many other villages all over England to give advice on setting up similar ventures.

Lynchmere is one of countless parish councils to respond to the idea of parish maps and village appraisals, and they did so in style. During the appraisal period (1989-91) they not only sent lengthy questionnaires to every household, and analysed and published the results, but also collected some 1,800 old photographs of local personalities and scenes, formed a Lynchmere Society and, on the 800th anniversary of Shulbrede Priory, put on the Lynchmere Pageant to celebrate the Village

92.   The Harting Minibus at the heart of South Harting.

Appraisal 'and as a thanksgiving for the place in which we live'. They produced a large-scale parish map marking every local feature, and this was eventually engraved on steel and erected at Shottermill Ponds near the war memorial. They learned a great deal about the parish, past and present (and its future hopes), and the appraisal committee in the guise of the Lynchmere Society continues the work, albeit at a slower pace. The appraisal itself makes intriguing reading as a portrait of a scattered parish. The parish council also issues a regular newsletter and a special 'Welcome to Lynchmere' leaflet for all newcomers.

Fernhurst, another parish council to issue regular newsletters, has just opened one of the country's few telecottages, after incorporating a feasibility study in the parish appraisal questionnaire. A telecottage is a place in the village where local people can train and/or work with computers and communications equipment, whether they simply want to learn how, or are running their own small businesses from home. This is very much the trend for the future and a very positive way of keeping villages alive with people working in the parish rather than commuting and using it only as a dormitory. Several villages are watching the venture with keen interest, especially those with village halls.

Yapton revived a local tradition in 1984, when six old trophies were rediscovered in the attic of the parish council's post-war chairman. His daughter, a parish councillor at the time of the discovery, resurrected the purpose of the trophies: the Yapton Walk, first held in 1932 but killed off by the war. The walk was an endurance test and the cups were presented to walkers who covered the greatest distance in seven hours. An incentive to beat the bounds?

Parish councils can be international, too. The idea of 'twinning' with a continental counterpart was rejected by the parish councils of **Upper Beeding** and **Bramber**. Instead, they got together and 'adopted' the village of Yobe in Somalia in 1985, setting up a trust with the aim of raising an annual £2,000 to help the work of a charity in upgrading the school, sinking water wells and providing knowledge on crop-growing. Closer to home, Upper Beeding has faced the problem of vandalism head on. As the parish council chairman Keith Nethercoate-Bryant explains, the idea arose when the parishes of Upper Beeding, Bramber and Steyning held a ceremony to open a long-awaited bypass. Nethercoate-Bryant was anxious that the opening should be by those who would benefit most in the future—the children. The proposal was accepted by the county council, which also donated trees for planting at the parish boundaries.

This joint event triggered off other ideas, including a joint meeting between the parish council and the school with the vicar, the local police, parents and teachers to talk about a recent spate of playground vandalism. The outcome was that the parish council established and paid for evening classes and extra-mural lessons for primary school children (with subjects such as chess, playing the accordion, swimming, gymnastics, cross-country running and knitting) on the principle that boredom breeds vandals. They also reckoned that involving the children in parish affairs at a young age might pay dividends and they devised community ventures such as tree-planting and sponsored village clean-ups. They continued the theme of having the children open this and that—starting with a new school extension, and then an adventure playground. The children were told that this playground was their own and that they had become its custodians, with the task of handing it on eventually to their own children in good condition. Suddenly there were 400 pairs of young eyes on the alert for vandals! The aim has been to encourage civic pride at an early age and motivate the children to accept responsibility for their own environment. And it works.

Other parish councils also involve local children. Just across the border, in East Sussex, Forest Row created a 'Youth Forum' as a sort of junior parish council in 1977, so successfully

93. *(Right)* The cover of Lynchmere parish
appraisal. Based on questionnaires delivered to
every household in the parish, to which 59 per
cent responded, the appraisal became the guide for
future parish council policy and also generated an
invaluable collection of memories and old
photographs.

· **Lynchmere** ·
· West Sussex ·

Village Appraisal &
Parish Map 1988 - 1990.

— Report —

94. *(Below)* Fernhurst Telecottage, a trend for the
future? Pictured at its official opening in 1993: the
Duke of Richmond (seated at the computer) and,
from left, Arthur Waitt (parish councillor and
chairman of the steering committee), Brigadier
Alan Findlay (West Sussex county councillor) and
Alec Fry (manager of the Telecottage).

that one of its members became a fully-fledged elected parish councillor at the age of 22. **Twineham** parish council is involving its primary school in a parish council centenary project with a joint exhibition on local history. **Hurstpierpoint** has quite elaborate plans for centenary celebrations and formed a special organising group well in advance.

Bersted hopes to celebrate the centenary with, at the least, a fête and a special reception: they are determined to make a bit of a splash in 1994. This is one of the new wave of 'proactive' parish councils: it owns and runs a community centre; it arranges for the local playbus to visit a particular estate in the parish on a weekly basis under a Care Network scheme; it has encouraged several neighbourhood watch schemes; it works closely with various amenity and youth groups and regularly enters the Best Kept Village competition. It is an ardent protector of its environment and firmly resisted a proposal for a huge housing estate on grade 1 agricultural land, while at the same time co-operating with the district council to find new sites for smaller groups of housing.

Another active parish council in a different way is **Worth**, a semi-rural parish, which must be unique for the amount and range of grants that it gives each year. It simply puts up posters saying, in effect, 'Money available: Who wants any?' and then works its way through all the applications. Some of the results have been half a euphonium for the Silver Band, a piano for the Ladies Choir, underwear for Chernobyl children, tents for the NTC, and all sorts of grants to local clubs, schools, churches, community centres and charities. Worth parish council has given over £100,000 in grants to local organisations in the past ten years. Their attitude is that no community functions well without a healthy selection of local organisations, and these need support in order to thrive—in most cases, they need money above all. Fund-raising is a continuous problem for them, and this is where an enlightened local authority can help. Worth recognised some ten years ago that many local bodies were being held back by lack of cash; it therefore made a positive decision to pursue a policy of giving grant aid to those organisations considered worthy of support, especially those that were going ahead with their projects whatever the problems—they were in need of just a bit of encouragement. 'Financial assistance was welcome, of course', explains the clerk, Keith Wall, 'but even more helpful, perhaps, was the knowledge that someone in authority appreciated their efforts to the extent of doing something concrete about it.'

No fewer than 63 town and parish councils in West Sussex marked the centenary of West Sussex County Council in 1989 by taking part in the planting of over 100 oak trees in towns and villages across the county. Local councils have always worked closely with the County Council and, in 1992, were parties to a pioneering Statement of Partnership in Local Government, setting out ways in which town and parish councils and the County Council work together for the benefit of the people of West Sussex.

Finally, in collecting material for this book from parish councils all over the county, the most inspiring response has been from **Patching**. Space does not allow a full reproduction of the story received from Patching's clerk but here is the gist of what they are achieving, and why.

Patching is one of the smallest parishes in West Sussex, in population (about 200) as well as in area. It was a parish meeting for many years, doing very little—to such an extent that the minutes of the 1926 meeting were not signed until 1944. Then it woke up to protest 'against the menacing attack on the liberty of the subject'—Worthing RDC's post-war housing plans. In 1946 Patching held its first meeting as a parish council.

In 1971 it began to discuss a proposed realignment of the A27 as a means of overcoming the 'rat run' through the village. And discuss and discuss, scheme after scheme. It was not

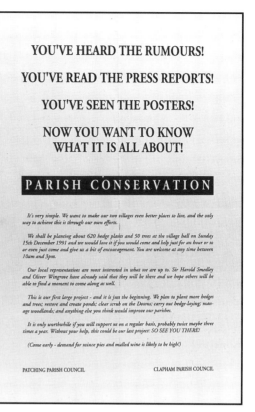

95 & 96. The Patching and Clapham initiative.

until the 1990s that the Patching Improvement scheme became a realistic possibility, and that prospect released a great creative burst within the parish council from 1991 onwards. It decided that it must get the residents of the parish to accept responsibility for the place where they lived and to commit themselves by giving of their time and effort. 'We want to make giving to the parish a matter of routine', explains the clerk, Robin Tilley, 'something that is an unquestioned way of life'.

In December 1991 they decided to plant some 640 hedging plants and trees around the hall's grounds. They advertised the event heavily and so many people turned out that they finished in an hour what had been expected to take all day. 'There were four things about that event which were useful. The first was realising how important it is to get across to people what is happening and when, and to raise it to a level in their consciousness that they actually do something about it. The second was appreciating that bribery has its uses: we offered all who came free mince pies and mulled wine. They all enjoyed it and it gave the event a party feel ... The third was taking down the names of everyone who came to help, on the basis that quite a few might have the germ of an inclination to help on other ideas if I nobbled them later. The fourth was getting to know what we were up against and the identities of those who can only see matters in terms of why things cannot be done rather than why they can be done.'

97.   Poster for Clapham and Patching weekend.

That last remark is perhaps the key to Patching, and certainly to Mr. Tilley, who is very against the excuse that, if a particular matter is not to your liking, it is someone else's fault and someone else's responsibility to put it right. For example, he is often told that, since it was the farmers who grubbed out all the hedges, then it is the farmers who should put them back. He disagrees. 'Whatever the rights and wrongs of it might have been, the simple fact is that if we want the hedges back, then it is up to us to replant them and look after them. It is unrealistic and probably unfair to expect the farmers (who have been pushed and pulled in all sorts of directions by different policies) suddenly to note the error of their ways and plant lots of hedges, which are of little use to them (however much they might or might not approve of them) and when they do not have the labour force to look after them properly. We now live in the village, and in the houses, where the agricultural work force used to live, and if we feel strongly enough about the issue, then let us make the effort to help the farmers and undertake the maintenance of the hedges that would have been our predecessors' roles. We should do it as a matter of course, without expecting any reward save the satisfaction of doing something worthwhile. It means giving, and not just taking.'

And they did. Quite apart from clearing one of the parish's oldest footpaths ('the parish whisky took a pounding') and holding an ambitious Village Weekend in August 1992, they got together a team of 14 volunteers to learn the art of hedge-laying. The training was sponsored by the parish council, which also bought some of the tools, and the team laid its first hedge in February 1993. During the following summer, seven of the hedge-layers were trained by the Agricultural Training Board in the proper use of chainsaws, and they intend also to become experts with tractor and flail, sympathetically used as an efficient way of maintaining hedges once laid.

The next project was the construction of a dew pond on Patching Hill as a wildlife habitat, to replace the many that have been lost. With the help of bribery (wine and sausage rolls), they persuaded 60 people to turn up and lend a hand, or just watch, in an operation involving two JCBs, a Hi-Mac, and a convoy of 20-ton lorries carrying 200 tons of clay and 20 round bales of straw. Next, they commissioned a general habitat survey of the parish, not just as a historical snapshot but also as the basis for identifying future projects. They are organising a guided nature walk, and a major tractor-and-trailer ride of three or four hours to beat the parish bounds.

98.   Patching Hill dewpond. Ron Olley handling the straw.

99.   Patching Hill dewpond. Spreading the plastic membrane, which was sandwiched between layers of straw.

100. Robin Tilley *(left)*, driving force behind the Patching initiative. With parish stalwarts Paul Kimber *(centre)* and Ed Bacon.

101. West Sussex County Council support for the Patching initiative. County councillor Sir Henry Smedley handing a cheque to Mike Cooper, chairman of the parish council in 1992.

And there is more. 'The Village Enhancement Scheme is another way of getting the parishioners, at least in the central part of the village, involved and thinking positively about the place where they live. The idea is to come up with lots of proposals—mostly modest but some major—which, if implemented, would have a significant beneficial impact on the village. For example, we can dig out all the blocked drains, repair and renew all the road verges, replace broken-down barbed wire fences with chestnut post-and-rail fences, use redundant land as wildlife areas and stick a bench there, renew the old village clock, put up our own signs to identify particular places before their names get forgotten and so on. I could go on,' says Mr. Tilley, and they certainly will.

Tilley has become an expert at tracking down advice and grants for their projects. His council is not afraid of spending money ('If our parishioners do not like what we are doing then they can say so, and ultimately get rid of us ... Between us we know all of them personally.') and believes that parish affairs should be a pleasure as well as a duty. They are now thinking of sponsoring events that their parishioners might enjoy. And they achieved a splendid attendance at the annual parish meeting by showing a video of the year's activities, which 'caused much amusement'.

It is not all amusement: indeed it is all hard work, and not free from controversy. 'We have to leave behind those who have been forced to admit that they oppose us because they want everything to "stay the same". The truth is that their inaction allows the inevitable changes that do occur, to do so without adequate checks. There are two certainties in life: death and change. We prefer not to fool ourselves that somehow or other we are exceptions to these certainties and to control those changes for the good of the parish, including the wildlife.'

And that is really what living in a parish is all about. Let Mr. Tilley have the last word by way of a challenge to all West Sussex parish councils in their centenary year:

'We say to people that if they feel powerless to help world problems, they can help where they live and actually make a difference: we call their bluff! In isolation our efforts may be pretty insignificant, but if our philosophy could fit in with other like-minded parishes, then it might not be.'

Bibliography

Arnold-Baker, Charles, *Local Council Administration* (3rd edition 1989, Longcross Press)

Godfrey, John, Leslie, Kim and Zeuner, Diana, *A Very Special County: West Sussex County Council, The First 100 Years* (1988, WSCC)

Jeffreys, Rees, *The King's Highway: An Historical and Autobiographical Record of the Developments of the past sixty Years* (1949, Batchworth Press)

Keith-Lucas, Bryan, and Richards, Peter G., *A History of Local Government in the Twentieth Century* (1978, George Allen & Unwin)

Margary, Harry (ed.), *250 Years of Map Making in Sussex 1575-1825* (1970, Phillimore)

Morrison Davidson, J., *The Villagers' Magna Charta: 'The Village for the Villagers'* (3rd edition 1895, William Reeves)

Nash, H. F. and Allport, J. S., *Parish Councils and Parish Meetings* (1895)

Redlich, Josef and Hirst, Francis W., *The History of Local Government in England* (1903; 2nd edition edited by Bryan Keith-Lucas 1970, Macmillan)

Smith, Allen, *A History of the County Surveyors' Society 1885-1985*

Index of Place Names

The index is divided into two sections: **1. Place names** (excluding references on maps and in tables) **2. General subjects** (including names of people). Page numbers in bold indicate illustrations.

General Index